FOURTH EDITION

INSTINCT COMBAT SHOOTING

Defensive Handgunning for Police

FOURTH EDITION

INSTINCT COMBAT SHOOTING

Defensive Handgunning for Police

CHUCK KLEIN

CRC Press
Taylor & Francis Group
Boca Raton London New York

CRC Press is an imprint of the
Taylor & Francis Group, an **informa** business

CRC Press
Taylor & Francis Group
6000 Broken Sound Parkway NW, Suite 300
Boca Raton, FL 33487-2742

Printed on acid-free paper
Version Date: 20160504

International Standard Book Number-13: 978-1-4987-6691-3 (Hardback)

Visit the Taylor & Francis Web site at
http://www.taylorandfrancis.com

and the CRC Press Web site at
http://www.crcpress.com

Printed and bound in the United States of America by Publishers Graphics, LLC on sustainably sourced paper.

To the Law Enforcement Officers who are challenged daily by

the whims of political correctness, while remaining ethical and honest,

as they brave omnipresent deadly evil.

Contents

Foreword

Since the mid-1950s, there has been a rise in popularity of combat match events as orchestrated by the International Practical Shooting Confederation (IPSC). The chief promulgator of this practice is its founder, Col. Jeff Cooper, USMC, Retired. Col. Cooper has a fine reputation as a gun writer and social commentator, and it is a reputation he fully deserves. In June of 1976, I graduated from Cooper's course, which I took directly under him in Washington County, Ohio, with a number of other law enforcement officers. As a combat martial arts teacher, I have always incorporated modern weaponry into my program, and at the time I felt that it was my responsibility to find out about any new developments that may have taken place in handgun technique since WWII.

Although I had been fully persuaded that the proven methods of the wartime masters (Col. Rex Applegate and Maj. William W. Fairbairn) were the proper methods for real-world combat shooting, I kept an open mind. Inevitably, I saw that, excellent as the "new technique" might have been for winning matches and competitive events, point firing, or as Chuck Klein, the pioneer of this method with a handgun calls it, *Instinct Combat Shooting*, was the only true combat technique for actual man-against-man close-quarter engagements where the outcome is life or death.

To be totally honest, I wasn't that surprised. Point firing developed as a result of direct and actual combat experience, and research into the phenomenon surrounding events in lethal confrontations.

Today's police-style competitive shooting, the so-called Weaver Stance and the use of the weapon's sights, is the standard. It is certainly the method in use in open competition, and perhaps this accounts for its popularity. Nevertheless, in actual close-quarters combat, the use of the weapon's sights is almost *never* appropriate, since the ranges are almost invariably close, that is, 3–20 feet. What is much more important is the psychophysical reactions of the human organism when confronting a deadly human adversary, which precludes the type of response that sighted shooting requires. This has been consistently proven in actual combat since the 1930s, and it is common knowledge among experienced law enforcement, protective service, and military trainers.

We who advocate instinctive or point firing do not say that the handgun's sights should never be used. We only remind those who will listen that their use—in combat—is necessarily limited to the relatively few situations in which the distances permit them to be employed. At the ranges (between 1 and 21 feet) where nearly all actual armed confrontations occur, certain things happen that prevent sighted firing:

- The onset of what psychologists call the "peripheral-optic dysfunction phenomena," which entails a tunnel vision lock on to the perceived lethal threat
- Auditory exclusion
- Time–space distortion
- The loss of the ability to render fine motor articulations in favor of gross body actions, as well as the natural inclination to crouch

Instinctive firing actually makes use of the naturally occurring phenomenon, and thus provides the shooter with a technique that is totally compatible with natural physiological response and psychological reaction. I have heard the idiotic criticism of instinctive firing—that man is not born with instincts (!), and therefore instinctive firing is useless. Instinctive firing is called what it is because it is so natural and so easily compatible with human response to deadly threat situations that it *feels* instinctive (as if the critics didn't know that is what is meant). "Directed firing" and the already alluded to "point firing" are terms synonymous with the basic technique.

The Israelis, the British, and the French teach this method of combat shooting to their military, counter-terrorist, and intelligence elites. In the System of Combat Martial Arts that I founded (AMERICAN COMBATO—Jen-Do-Tao), it is this shooting technique that is taught in our weapons curriculum for the handgun.

I first discovered Chuck Klein's *Instinct Combat Shooting: Defensive Handgunning for Police* in the late 1980s. I have since recommended it in my monthly column "Defensive Combat" that appears in *Petersen's Handguns for Sport and Defense* magazine and have placed it on recommended reading lists for students and instructors in and out of law enforcement. I am delighted to recommend this new, expanded edition of Chuck's book. Along with Applegate's *Kill Or Get Killed*, Fairbairn's *Shooting to Live*, Jordan's *No Second Place Winner*, Gaylord's *Handgunner's Guide*, and

Weston's *Combat Shooting for Police*, I consider *Instinct Combat Shooting* by Chuck Klein to be a valuable reference and training guide.

Read—and study—this important book. Should your life ever be on the line, you will doubtlessly say a prayer of thanks for having done so.

Bradley J. Steiner*

---

* Bradley J. Steiner (http://www.americancombato.com/professorbradle_118155.cfm) is a combat martial arts professor and teaches police, military, bodyguards and civilians at his Academy of Self-Defense in Seattle, Washington, United States (206/523-8642). He is president of the International Combat Martial Arts Federation, Founder of AMERICAN COMBATO, former Washington State Director of American Society of Law Enforcement Trainers, and author of many books on close combat that are in use throughout the world. He has been a teacher for 28 years.

Preface

The second to last thing a morally responsible, prudent person wants to do is kill another human being regardless of how reprehensible, villainous or dangerous that person might be. The last thing this morally responsible, prudent person wants to do is be killed by that reprehensible, villainous and dangerous person.

Klein's 1st law of survival

Since the introduction of the concepts taught in this book, police agencies all over the world have adopted the methods of *Instinct Combat Shooting* with a handgun. Sometimes called "point shooting," a somewhat ambiguous term, this technique of firefight survival has universally taken hold after many years of ridicule and doubt by some of the old school instructors— way back when many officers charged with police training scoffed at the thought of ever firing a shot without the proper "sight picture," especially with a pistol or revolver. Testimony of survivors of shootouts and careful analysis of close-quarter firefights have proven that shooting instinctively is not only extremely fast, but equally accurate under the pressure of a close-quarter gun battle. In addition, court decisions such as *Popow v. City of Margate*, 476 F.Supp. 1237 (N.J. 1979), mandate officers must be trained in all phases of handgun use, including moving target techniques. Impacting a moving target while trying to maintain a "sight picture" is truly a lucky hit. The *Popow* decision made it clear that police officers must have job-related training.

The former and common PPC (Practical Pistol Course, developed in the 1930s) is no longer reality. Studies of recent officer-involved shootings have shown that most firefight situations occur at close range, in a very short time span and under limited light conditions. Circumstances the PPC did not address. This book picks up where others have left off in teaching street survival and includes moving target instruction, which exchanges luck for skill during close-quarter combat applications.

The methods shown here are not for the novice. Basic abilities of bull's-eye shooting, including accepted breathing, grip, and trigger control are prerequisites to make effective use of these techniques.

Most people can shoot a handgun as all that is required is the pulling of the trigger. However, not all can score well much less hit the intended target under adverse conditions. It is hoped that the reader will benefit from the contents of this book and thus increase his or her chances of survival should a real-life firefight ever be encountered.

For those who carry a handgun for defensive purposes, there is no such thing as too much of the right kind of practice. *Instinct Combat Shooting: Defensive Handgunning for Police* presents the correct methods and ways to practice to be a survivor when time, distance, and lives are at stake.

Instinct Combat Shooting is not a panacea—a handgun tactic that covers all combat conditions. The author is not in any way suggesting or advocating its use for long-range shooting with a handgun. It is, however, championed as the fastest and best method for distances from contact out to about 7 yards—the accepted gap at which a knife wielder has the advantage before an armed person can react, draw, and fire. The concepts and practices defined, described, and demonstrated in this text are intended for surviving close-quarter combat conditions—distances where the combatants are less than 7 yards (21 feet) apart.

Survival depends upon paranoia becoming prudence long before sixth-sense warnings, flashing knives, or flying bullets.

Klein's 16th law of survival

Focusing on this sights, this officer can't possibly
determine which of these rioters is the
greatest threat to him.

About the Author

Chuck Klein, in addition to duties as a full-time certified police officer for Woodlawn and Terrace Park, Ohio, also served with the Switzerland County, Indiana Sheriff's Office, was police photography instructor for the Police Academy in Norwood, Ohio, and a staff instructor for the Tactical Defense Institute (www.tdiohio.com). Though not an attorney, he holds a bachelor of law degree from the Blackstone School of Law and is an active member of the International Association of Law Enforcement Firearms Instructors (IALEFI). Klein's byline has appeared in national magazines, including, but not limited to, *Law & Order, Street Rod Action, Old Car News, Classic Car, P.I. Magazine, Police Magazine, Law Officer Magazine, Gun Week, Guns & Ammo,* and *American Police Beat.* Contact and additional information may be found on his website www.chuckklein.com.

Though Klein didn't invent instinct shooting by any definition, he was one of the pioneers of instinct shooting with a *handgun*; a concept that is now taught worldwide by some of the most progressive police agencies.

1

Historical Background

INSTINCT SHOOTING

The first handheld, projectile-discharging weapons had no sights at all and some, a la the blunderbuss with its belled muzzle, had no sight plane to install sights on. Many shotgun shooters have always hunted and fired upon moving clay targets or live birds, sans sights. However, not all trap and skeet shooters utilize *instinct* (sightless shooting) methods—some practice the lead and follow-through form. The lead and follow-through is fine when the target direction and speed are known or can be determined upon first visual contact. Of course, in human combat, it is not possible to predict where the target is going next. Furthermore, the lead and follow-through technique does not take into account stationary targets and thus does not lend itself to handgun shooting. Enter *Instinct Combat Shooting*, that is, instinct shooting with a handgun under human combat conditions where life and death is decided not only by split seconds but in attention spans.

Instinct Combat Shooting is defined as follows:

> The act of operating a HANDGUN by focusing on the target, as opposed to the sights, and instinctively coordinating the hand and mind to cause the HANDGUN to discharge at a time and point that ensures interception of the projectile with the target.

Instinct shooting is not new as there are numerous books and articles on the subject, although most are slanted toward shotgun use on clay or live birds. However, many of the same techniques apply and the serious instinct shooter is encouraged to read and study the works of other authors such as *Instinct Shooting* by Mike Jennings. This 1959 publication tells the story of Lucky McDaniel, another pioneer of instinct shooting with a rifle.

Rifle combatants had little need for sightless shooting due to the great distances usually associated with single projectile-discharging long arms. However, in the mid-1960s, the U.S. Army initiated a program to teach selected infantry troops how to shoot instinctively with the then relatively new M16. To shoot instinctively, it was historically believed that the weapon must be supported by both hands plus at two contact points, namely, the shoulder and the cheek—a method that excludes handguns.

Most other instinct rifle shooting was limited to trick shot artists. With the exception of trick shooters such as the late and extraordinarily talented Ed McGivern, instinct shooting with a handgun was not considered a feasible means of protecting one's life. An early attempt to explain the use of instinctively shooting handguns was published in a feature article in *Law & Order* magazine (*Instinct Combat Shooting*, Chuck Klein, October 1971). For the next 15 years, except with the support of a select few such as the late Col. Rex Applegate, the concept of instinct shooting with a handgun was attacked, vilified, and ridiculed by most police agencies. McGivern certainly was a master of instinct shooting with a handgun, but nowhere in his 500-page book, *Fast and Fancy Revolver Shooting*, does he tell *how* he does it. He either couldn't or wouldn't explain *how* he did it—how to shoot instinctively with a handgun.

Shotgun and military combat rifle shooters practice shooting, sans sights, at moving targets. However, *instinct combat shooters* need to be able to hit a moving target while on the move themselves. Sighted fire is not possible especially when the movement of the target is erratic. The human eye and mind—while trying to align sights or even just the front sight—cannot make the rapid calculations necessary to cause the *handgun* to discharge at a time and point that ensures interception of the projectile with the target. This function of eye/mind/hand timing is done simultaneously and instinctively just like striking a ball with a tennis racquet. Imagine trying to put sights on a tennis racquet.

In the 1960s, with the help of the late, eminent Dr. Bruce Wolff, O.D., I began studying the notion that the contact points could be just finger placement on the weapon's stocks—in addition to the well-honed basics of trigger control, constant grip pressure, and general handgun discipline.

The author's early experiments utilizing the totally inadequate factory-issue stocks of then state-of-the-art revolvers proved to be discouraging. However, when form-fitting and hand-filling custom grips were installed, the results were very much in line with the hypothesis. Skeet and trap shooters have known since the beginning of the sport that a proper fitting stock is paramount to shot placement. Therefore, and in order to develop a natural pointing handgun, the stocks must also fit the shooter.

THE INVENTORS

Though Bill Fairbairn and Eric Sykes are generally credited with being the fathers of instinct shooting, I have never read anything on exactly how they do it. Fairbairn and Sykes, in their treatise, *Shooting to Live*, championed instinctive handgun shooting for close-quarter combat shooting, ca. 1942. However, much has been learned since then. The following is a point-by-point comparison of their teachings to the now accepted methods for improving officers' chances of firefight survival.

Fairbairn and Sykes suggest the purpose of a pistol is a one-hand handgun. The only time they tout two-handed shooting is for distances of greater than 10 yards. The teaching today is toward two-handed use not only for control of the shot placement, but also the two-handed hold (when possible) that is far more secure should a surprise suspect grapple for the weapon.

The *shooting to live* premise is based on "three essential points"

1. *Extreme speed, both in drawing and firing*: This is confusing because they suggest that the handgun of preference is the semiauto carried in condition 3 (chamber empty, safety off). They suggest that students should be able to fire their first shot in 1/3 of a second. From the ready position that might be possible, but from a holstered weapon—especially with a gun that is in condition 3, I defy anyone to reach that goal. Besides, it required two hands just to get the pistol into condition 1. Thus if the non-shooting hand is injured or busy repelling an attacker, the hand won't be available to ready the pistol.
2. *Instinctive, as opposed to deliberate aim*: They give no instruction on how to achieve this other than to instruct a student to "concentrate

his gaze on the center of the [target]." This is a good start, however, and contrary to "instinctive" shooting, they insist that the student incorporate a number of rigid body positions, including

a. Rigid straight arm. Time taken to get into any predetermined physical position is the time your adversary has to win the firefight. *Instinct Combat Shooting* is not conditioned on any special positioning other than a hand on the gun and pointed to where the eyes are looking.

b. Square stance to the point of resquaring the feet if the need to engage a second target is presented. Again, forced body positions are time wasted.

c. Covering the target with the gun. This is most difficult, if not impossible, to do instinctively as the master eye and the non-dominate eye will force the student to waste time in trying to determine if the target is, in fact, covered. This is not instinct shooting inasmuch as the shooter consciously pulls the trigger— *not* when his brain/eye tell him to—but upon the mechanical positioning of when the gun is covering the target. If shooting at a moving target, the gun may never cover the target long enough for the conscious brain to tell the trigger finger to pull. The time it takes to realize the target is covered by the gun and send that message to the brain, which must then resend that information to the trigger finger, is measurable.

d. Controlling the trigger by applying pressure with all the fingers— not just the trigger finger. Modern techniques have dispelled this "lemon squeeze" type of trigger control. The gun should be gripped firmly while the trigger finger pulls straight back in a deliberate—nonjerking—rapid and smooth motion.

e. Place one foot forward of the other. Again, real *Instinct Combat Shooting* is dependent on the eye, hand, mind coordination and has nothing whatsoever to do with body positions. You can be lying flat on your back and still effectively shoot instinctively.

f. The authors of *Shooting to Live* champion the use of the "close-hip" position for shooting in very close-quarters such as grappling distance. There are so many positions for so many conditions that it is impossible to shoot instinctively—that is, the time it takes to assess the situation and then get into position will be time for your attacker to win the battle.

3. Practice under circumstances, which approximate as nearly as possible to actual fighting conditions. No argument here.

They suggest that the semiauto can be fired at "far greater speed." Obviously, they were not aware of Ed McGivern's experiments of the 1930s where Mr. McGivern was able to operate a revolver at speeds up to six shots in 2/5 of a second.

Fairbairn and Sykes considered 50% hits on a man size target at distances of 3–6 yards to be sufficient for qualification. In other words, your chances of survival are only 50% in a close-quarter combat battle. Any student of mine, at those distances who expects to survive a close-quarter firefight, better have a 100% hit rate.

Other historical instinct shooters such as Annie Oakley, Frank Butler, and Robert Churchill were extraordinarily talented, but they were shooting long guns and failed to record their methods.

2

Hardware

WEAPON CHOICE

First and foremost, use only quality firearms. To be proficient at any form of handgun shooting, you must consume many rounds of ammunition and poorly made guns just won't stand up. The old adage "you get what you pay for" holds doubly true for firearms. Quality is primarily due to three factors: the superiority of the steel, the degree of tempering of the steel, and the fit of the parts. Choose a gun with the history of and reputation for long-term reliable function. The extra hundred dollars or so you spend now will more than pay for itself if your cheap substitute fails at a life-threatening moment or if you have to replace the cheapie because it wore out during practice.

The actual choice of size, both physical and caliber, is whatever is most comfortable. A .44 Magnum, or even a .357 Magnum, that is not a pleasure to shoot is definitely not the gun to rely on. The same goes for the physical size of the handgun though custom-made stocks can make a larger gun feel smaller and vice versa. A few well-placed shots from a small caliber weapon are far better than a whole magazine of poorly placed shots from a magnum. Additionally, and more significantly, a firearm that is difficult or torturous to shoot will negate the tendency to practice.

Stainless steel weapons have come a long way since their debut in the early 1960s. The first-generation pieces had problems with tempering and were thus prone to premature wear and failure. Modern stainless steel firearms are both durable and practical for officers who may encounter adverse weather conditions. Heavy use, which would wear the finish from standard blued guns, is not a problem with SS. The same applies to polymer or alloy frame guns. Vast improvements over the years have proved their mettle. At least 600 rounds per year of practice plus hundreds of dry firings will take its toll on any handgun, but quality begets reliability.

Revolver or semiautomatic? Volumes have been written on the merits and shortcomings of both. However, in the last few years, advances have been made in design and function of both semiautos and the cartridges they digest. Suffice it to say that weight, size, steel type, or caliber is a personal matter; only the carrier has the right to decide. The primary criterion is that a self-defense firearm be of the type that doesn't require both hands or extraneous actions to get off a shot. For example, the 1911 style handguns that are carried in condition 1 (chamber loaded, hammer cocked, and safety on) meet that standard. A first-shot double-action gun that requires a slight change of hand positioning for follow-up single-action shots doesn't. Many current generation autoloaders, such as Glock or Sig Sauer, do not require user-operated safeties to keep the weapon from accidental firing. The downside of semiautos will always be jams and magazine releases that can inadvertently be activated, but these maladies are no more prevalent than a high primer is to locking up a revolver. Practice at clearing such gridlocks is a key to successfully finishing a firefight.

The critical decisive factor is what do you feel most comfortable and confident with? If, when you reach for that ultimate tool of last resort, what comes to mind? What would you like to have in your hand at that time? Is it the familiarity of your old reliable snub-nose revolver or the large caliber Glock or even your .32 PPK that prints where you look under all conditions? The answer to that question is what you should practice with and carry. This is not to say you can't become proficient with more than one firearm; just make sure your brain is in revolver mode if today you're carrying a revolver.

AMMUNITION

Practice ammunition, manufacture and type, should be whatever you are going to carry. However, it is advisable to use light loads until you have the fundamentals of trigger control, grip, etc., down pat. Then you can and should practice with the full loads you plan to carry to familiarize yourself with their noise, recoil, and accuracy.

Your life depends on the ammunition you select for your personal defense; be sure it performs well in your particular weapon. Though most loads will function uniformly in the same model of firearm, there are exceptions, and group size varies among different brands. Also, just like gun size, weight and caliber are matters of personal preference. Certain levels of noise and muzzle blast that various cartridges produce might be considered unacceptable to some.

Use only quality factory-loaded ammunition. Reloads from your department armorer or neighborhood buddy are not recommended for reliable life dependence performance, not to mention liability problems should you end up in court over a lethal force incident. The number of misfires or other quality control problems of factory loads is infinitesimal in comparison to the millions of rounds produced.

The case/bullet/load combination that groups best for you and for your particular handgun is the only round that you should carry and use for practice. Try not to get brainwashed by the claims of some new "hot shot" cartridge that exits the test barrels at a zillion feet per second and mushrooms to the size of a fist. If it shoots three foot groups for you, it's advisable to pass it up for the old reliable that hits where you hold. Again, the old adage applies: "A few well-placed shots...whole magazine of poorly...."

HANDGUN STOCKS

The stocks are the single most important piece of equipment on the handgun. They must fit your hand in such a way that every time you place your hand on them, your grip will be the same. In other words, your middle, ring, and little finger will wrap around to the same place on the opposite side of the stock, your thumb will lock down on the same location, thus allowing your trigger finger to place itself in the same position on the trigger. This applies to *Instinct Combat Shooting* as well as aimed fire. The difference is during aimed bull's eye shooting, you have time to adjust your hand position before commencing fire.

As you learned in basic range instruction, the pressure of your grip must be consistent in order to score consistently. The same principle applies to the placement of your fingers on the stocks. If the placement of the hand on the grip and the pressure of the fingers is constant and consistent, then the shots have to go in the same place. Move a finger or change the tension of the hold and the placement of the shot will be affected. During target shooting when you have an abundance of time to align sights and thus compensate for a shift of hand placement, acceptable scores can be realized. However, in *Instinct Combat Shooting* where there is no time and mechanical sights are not utilized, the positioning of the digits is of great importance. If you can't withdraw your weapon with the hands in the same place every time, then you're not ready for *Instinct Combat Shooting*.

The best way to get stocks to fit your hand is to make them yourself. Of course, most shooters don't have either the time or the ability to do this, though most oversize factory grips can be reshaped easily with a few wood rasps and a little sandpaper. The next best stocks come from reputable specialized custom stock makers. Luckily, most modern made handguns stocks (or off-the-shelf replacement grips) are very well made for consistent and workable hold.

Some of the new innovations in composition stock material have yielded many benefits for the handgunner. No longer are you limited to walnut or hard rubber. Several of the gun manufacturers have begun to offer form-fitting grips as a standard part of their weapon. Other makers are producing polymer frame arms where the frame and grip are integral and thus, modifications are limited, but not impossible.

In addition to the fit of the stock, it is imperative that the stocks do not interfere with loading, holstering, weapon withdrawal, or any other critical life-defending function.

The stocks on this Smith and Wesson M19 "Combat Magnum," which were custom-made to facilitate the placement of fingers and palm with judicious use of grooves and indentations. Putting your hand in the same place on the stock every time is very important in: you can place your shots in the same location consistently. Successful Instinct Combat Shooting requires the barrel–axis relationship to be in sync with eye-hand coordination. To put it another way, if the axis of the barrel is not aligned with where your hand is pointing (the target your eyes are focused on), the shot will be errant.

Because some manufacturers, such as this Glock M36, have integrated the frame with the stocks, restocking is not possible. However, careful filing and sanding can improve your grip. Here the owner has reduced the length of pull (distance from the backstrap to the trigger) to compensate for short fingers. The polymer frame/stock is easy to reconfigure— just be sure you don't remove too much material as replacement frames are expensive!

HOLSTERS

Critical to holster design is the ability to place the hand and fingers on the stocks in a way to not require any changes or shifting of digits (trigger finger excepted) once the firearm is being moved into battery. A properly designed and utilized holster will allow the shooter to rapidly seize the firearm, remove it, and bring it into the shooting position with the hand and fingers properly placed. In practice, if when the gun reaches battery, the sights are not lined up without having to shift or change your grip, something ain't right: the holster, the stocks, or your technique is amiss. Though *Instinct Combat Shooting* precludes the use of physical or laser sights—they are beneficial in dry-fire/practice exercises to check your alignment.

Stocks and holsters, for economic reasons, are generally made with the one-size-fits-all style. If the shooter wants to use the crouch or semicrouch shooting position, he/she should not begin the crouch movement until the weapon has cleared the holster. In the final phase of weapon removal, the entire unit—hand, gun, and arm, clear of the holster—continues moving toward the target until the unit discharge of the shot.

During *Instinct Combat Shooting* circumstances, the discharge occurs when the firearm comes to a stop against the non-shooting hand, or as in single handed control, at the limit of its forward travel. It is at this point and not an instant sooner or later, that the officer should fire a shot if he or she has already made the decision to shoot.

Holsters, like the firearms they retain, must be of high quality. Firm, rigid or semirigid, well-fitting rigs with a belt loop the size of the belt are a must. Except for certain undercover operatives, soft holsters that do not allow the user to redeposit their gun without the use of a second hand are not recommended. With the exception of uniformed officers, who must carry their handgun in the open and thus need security devices to keep unauthorized persons from gaining control of the weapon, all others should stay away from holsters that contain thumb snaps or similar controls. If you carry off duty or while in plain/undercover clothes, then you don't need to be fumbling for thumb breaks or other innovative security devices. Your holster should be of sufficient fit and quality that it will hold your weapon under all conditions. Pull-thru snaps that release by pulling the weapon out in the normal manner are the exception. There are many quality rigs available today that meet these requirements; try different ones to discover what fits you and then practice with it.

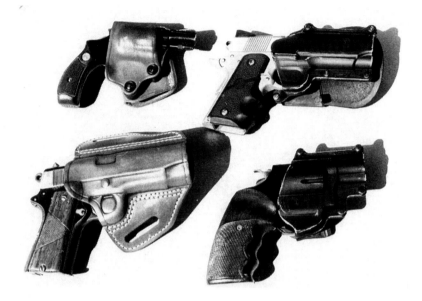

Selection of reliable holsters.

3

Safety Measures/Lead Poisoning

COMMON SENSE

If the situation demands that you approach a scene with your weapon in the ready position, place your trigger finger outside the trigger guard. The advantages of this practice are multiple. First, if an assailant should grab your handgun in a surprise move, he will not be able to wrest it from you by breaking the finger caught inside the trigger guard. Second, if you should stumble or fall, the muscle tensing reaction will not cause you to pull the trigger and perhaps injure an innocent person.

The practice of placing the finger above and alongside the trigger housing is also an acceptable safe carry method. However, it takes two movements to place your finger on the trigger should a shot be necessary, that is, to move the finger down and in, though the time involved in this additional movement is negligible inasmuch as the time is less than going from completed draw or the chest-ready position to battery (the decision to shoot has already been made). The placement of the finger in the same location on the trigger every time is just as important as the placement of any other digit. The shooter is advised to use and practice whatever method works best.

Of course, if you have identified a perpetrator as one who must be contained at the point of a gun, then your firearm will no longer be in the ready position but will actually be pointed at the target and you will be justified in keeping your finger on the trigger. The trigger finger is never placed on the trigger unless your target has been identified and you are justified in pointing a weapon at that target and are ready to shoot the subject target if necessary.

PRACTICE

Dry-firing is one of the most effective methods for learning any shooting discipline. Of course, handling firearms while not on the range requires the utmost in precautions—*the gun must be empty*. Good habits breed safety. If you are removing your carry arm for any reason other than to protect your life, store it away, or live-fire practice, *remove all ammunition*. Whether practicing in your home or office, be absolutely sure the gun is empty of all ammunition—especially the round in the chamber of a semiauto—even if the semiauto has a magazine disconnect. One of the best "habits" to get into when practicing is to say out loud—every time you pick the gun up: "The gun is empty." Saying it out loud, even if you are alone, helps jar the mind to the reality of what you are about to do. This also applies to when you reload the gun, that is, say out loud: "The gun is loaded."

Most modern handguns of quality will not be harmed by dry-firing, contrary to what many so-called gun experts have said in the past. As long ago as July 14, 1970, Smith & Wesson issued a written statement that said, in part: "Dry-firing will have no adverse effects on our handguns." The display card found in many gun stores admonishing: "People who know guns don't snap them" must only apply to the cheapies.

Another practical method to enhance your proficiency is to carry your gun in your hand for an hour or so each day. Familiarizing yourself with the feel of your life-saver is akin to football players and other professionals who carry the tools of their trade around while conducting unrelated duties. Your personal survival device should become so well known to your hand that no matter how you pick it up, it should automatically end up in the correct hand position.

Proper attire for the range includes hearing and eye protection plus a cap and long sleeve shirt to minimize lead contamination.

LEAD POISONING

A generation or so, ago, police officers were lucky if they shot once a year. Any practice between "qualifications" meant shooting solid lead "wadcutter" reloads. A few years later, it was determined that it was best to shoot what you carry for qualifications as well as all practice sessions. By the start of the 1990s in response to litigation fears, many departments began requiring monthly practice. Most factory ammunition is copper jacketed and, as the incorrect thinking of the time went, lead poisoning was eliminated—it was no longer a concern. Jacketed bullets most certainly spew lead particles upon impact with steel backstops, but the amount of this projectile disintegration borne residue is not as significant as the lead dust sprayed into the air—at arm's length to the shooter—upon discharge of the cartridge.

Today, ammo, in relation to cost-of-life indexes, is cheap. The watchword has become burn more powder. And, with burning powder comes the risk of toxic lead exposure. Also, with gratitude to the NRA, there are now many, many instructors who log hours and hours of range time.

Range officers, instructors, and beat officers, due mostly to increased firing line time and quantities of rounds fired, are exposed to greater amounts of toxic pollutants than ever before. The most dangerous of these toxins is lead. Not the lead bullet/pellets, per se, but the lead compounds sprayed into the air with the firing of the primer.

LEAD SOURCES

Lead (chemical symbol: Pb) is everywhere. Though it is heavier than air, it is in the air we breathe due to the inherent dust stirred up by moving objects (people, fan exhaust blades, ambient air movement). Lead is used in roofing materials, electric cable coverings, storage batteries, and radiation shields (dental/medical offices). It is also used in vulcanizing rubber, making glass, rust-resistant paints, insecticides, dyes, and, until the 1980s, gasoline. Lead, in dust form, accumulates in the human body, because it is one of the few ingredients not eliminated via kidney, liver, or other methods of waste removal functions. Lead damages red blood cells (hemolysis—rupturing of red blood cells) and causes degeneration of nerve cells in the brain.

If one were to, say, swallow a lead bullet, it would most likely pass through the digestive system as a solid nondigestible item with little or no adverse effects. If it doesn't pass, it can be removed surgically. If not removed, it will, in time, eat its way through wherever it is lodged, causing massive internal damage. However, tiny doses of lead, ingested through respiration or digestion, accumulate over a long period of time and do get into the blood. If the lead particles continue to accumulate, death will eventually result.

With the exception of lead-free cartridges, projectiles are made up of lead, copper, zinc, and antimony. The common properties of a primer are copper, zinc, lead antimony, barium, lead styphnate, and tetrazene. Unless the bullet is totally encased in a nonlead product (copper), elemental lead is shaved as it passes through the barrel and then dispersed into the air.

When this bullet impacts with a steel backstop, it breaks up, throwing more lead into the air and onto the ground. This form of lead, in its elemental state, is not the major concern. Elemental lead, in the form of dust from the fragmented bullets (after hitting steel backing plates), and shavings from the barrel are mostly a problem for clean-up crews at firing ranges.

It's the compound leads that are vaporized and formed by the burning powder that are of greatest risk to shooters and range officers. These dangerous gases come from two sources. First, the burning powder sears the base of the lead projectile, causing lead gases to be expelled with the powder residue. It is this compounded lead, along with the second source, the vaporized lead and lead styphnate (from the discharge of the primer), which possesses the greatest danger to those on the shooting line.

It has always been known that long-term and/or short intense exposure to lead particles and dust can cause lead poisoning. Until recently, the effect of the sports of shooting and reloading and required certification/ practice for most police officers to incidence of lead poisoning has been ignored. Reports of toxic levels of lead in police officers assigned to range duty, including one recent death, have raised the awareness. Perhaps, it's time for the police and civilian instructors and frequent shooters to take note.

Lead, when introduced into the human blood stream, is a most toxic substance. Even the tiniest amount, 1/2 of 1/10 (.05) of one grain, dissolved in your blood can produce adverse reactions. Though most cases of plumbism (lead poisoning) are treatable, the treatment, like the cumulative toxic condition, takes a long time. If you have had or are experiencing any of the symptoms described in the succeeding text, it might be best to re-examine your shooting/gun/ammunition handling practices and be tested by a doctor.

We all learned the lesson of wearing hearing protection from the older shooters who go around saying "huh" a lot. Those who lost an eye are testimony to the prudence of shooting glasses. Let's hope today's heavy shooters aren't the lead poisoning lesson for the next generation. If you're around the range a lot, be it indoor or outdoor, or you handle fired cases, take precautions and encourage your range officers to set the example.

SYMPTOMS OF LEAD POISONING

Some symptoms may be subtle or indicative of other disorders including, but not limited to, stress or mental illness. Everyone has occasional headaches, sleep loss, and fatigue. Consistent symptoms should be a trigger that something is seriously wrong. The "catch-22" is that brain dysfunction or short-term memory problems might contribute to the inability to self-diagnose the seriousness of the symptom. Making one's spouse, partner, or significant other aware of these symptoms and perform short regular mental/memory tests might rectify the problem.

- Loss of memory and difficulty in concentrating. This is usually the first noticeable symptom.
- Fatigue in various degrees. This includes pallor, malaise, loss of appetite, irritability, and sudden behavioral changes.
- Insomnia, which may exacerbate fatigue.
- Headaches accompanied by depression.
- Neurological disorders such as muscle spasms.
- Mental disorders such as depression, psychoses, and convulsions.
- Brain deterioration; this is the most serious condition inasmuch as damage is not treatable and usually is permanent. Symptoms include limb paralysis, confusion, disorientation, coordination problems, and/or insanity.
- Amyotrophic lateral sclerosis (degenerative disease of the nerve cells that controls the muscles).
- Digestive difficulties and abdominal pains, with or without weight loss.
- Elevated blood pressure.
- Joint pains.
- Anemia (hemolysis—rupturing of red blood cells).
- Menstrual irregularity and decreased fertility.
- Kidney and/or liver damage.
- Sore or bleeding gums marked by a blue line at the junction of the teeth and gums.

Please note that symptoms and the severity of such are different in each person. Also, because lead poisoning symptoms are so varied and mimic other maladies, it is difficult to self-diagnose. Though other heavy metals such as gold and iron are present (and needed) in the human body, lead, in any amount, is not. Lead is toxic to all persons but is easily detected with a BLL (blood lead level) test available at most clinics, hospitals, or doctor's offices. Lead contamination on clothing, skin, or other objects can be tested for with test kits such as the HybriVet Systems lead check swabs. These analysis tools are inexpensive and are readily available from most paint supply stores.

SUGGESTED PREVENTIVE MEASURES

Here, like most things in life, common sense is the key. If lead is a toxin and part of your job involves being exposed to it, then keeping the workspace and your personal gear clean is tantamount to avoiding the dangers. Preventive measures are always better than undergoing treatment. Because symptoms tend to come on slowly and affect short-term memory, infected persons might not be able to recognize the onset of the conditions until serious damage occurs. Practice the following:

- Blow your nose after shooting.
- After any shooting or reloading session, wash your hands and face before eating or smoking.
- Wash hair before bed. Lead particles in the hair can transfer to the pillow and thus be ingested during sleep.
- Use lead-free primers (though not as popular as the common lead styphnate primers, they are available from most makers). This might sound like a simple solution, but the added cost of these nontraditional rounds might create budget problems for the department. Also, as with any new product, it should have a few years of testing and field experience before being relied upon for officer survival. Have your doctor test you for lead levels as part of your regular check-ups.
- Change out of your shooting clothes and footgear to avoid contaminating car, home, or office—especially important if you have small children.

- Appoint a spouse, partner, parent, C.O. to ask and record the answers to a series of questions—on a weekly basis. The questions might include:
  - What did you have for: (most recent meal)?
  - What is your mother's maiden name, your social security number, and yesterday's date?
  - Complete the following equation: $5 + 3 + 7 - 6 \times 2 - 17 = (1)$
  - Have you had any trouble sleeping or concentrating?
  - Have you experienced any recent joint pains, headaches, memory loss, or suppressed appetite?

The answers to these (or similar) questions should flow easily and quickly. The observer should note any non- or incorrect answers and if these inconsistencies continue, lead toxicity test might be in order.

SUGGESTED RANGE RULES AND PROCEDURES

Most of these preventive measures are very inexpensive—especially when compared to the cost of officer rehabilitation after contamination.

- Signs posted to forbid consumption of food, tobacco, beverages, and cosmetics being carried into, stored, or consumed on the firing range. Anyone exposed to lead by handling fired cases or shooting should wash their hands and face before eating, drinking, or smoking.
- Plastic bags should be available for shooters to place their contaminated clothes for transport to their home laundry facilities.
- Shooters using the kneeling or prone position should cover the ground with heavy paper.
- Range maintenance workers should be required to change clothes, shower, and shampoo daily. Separate lockers should be provided to keep clean street clothes separate from contaminated work clothes.
- Encourage the use of lead-free ammunition.
- After each use, the range floor should be vacuumed with a unit designed for collecting lead. Dry sweeping should never be practiced.
- On indoor ranges, the ventilation system should be in operation during all shooting, clean-up, and maintenance operations.

- Range officers, maintenance workers, clean-up crews, and anyone who engages in shooting activities on a substantial basis should wear breathing masks or respirators.
- Consider having the range professionally cleaned. Some companies specialize in lead reclamation even by "mining" lead from outdoor earth banks. Depending upon the market value of reclaimed lead and copper, this might be a source of income for the department. Searching the Internet for "lead reclamation" should produce a number of companies in this field.
- These same high exposure officers, workers, and shooters should have a BLL test every 6 months. The BLL is measured in micrograms per deciliter (μg/dL). Though everyone has some level of lead in their blood, there is no acceptable level, but the current thinking is that 40 μg/dL in adults (25 μg/dL in children) is usually associated with acute symptoms. This level is not an absolute in all persons and might be adjusted after further study, that is, the threshold has been reduced from the 1970 level of 60 μg/dL.
- Wear breathing masks (rated for lead dust) if you are going to spend much time on the range—special attention instructors. It might seem silly to wear breathing masks, but remember how "silly" it was to wear ear protection 20–30 years ago?

CORRECTIVE MEASURES

If caught in time, lead poison is treatable. Though there is no cure for lead poisoning, proper care can reduce mortality. The primary treatment must be removal of the poison-causing conditions, that is, if you shoot, handle firearms, ammunition, or components or clean firing ranges stay away from those exposure locations. Medical remedies include administration of chelation drugs, which bind to the heavy metal particles, allowing for elimination through the digestive tract. The problem with the chelation treatment is that the drug not only cleans the body of lead, but also of other heavy metals (such as gold, copper, zinc, etc.) which are required, in trace amounts, for normal body functioning. Usually, over time and in as lead-free environment as possible, the symptoms will abate. Caught-in-time is the key inasmuch as if the condition has reached the stage of degeneration of nerve cells in the brain or if the liver has been destroyed, death might be unavoidable. This is not to say that even if caught-in-time, one is "home-free." The damage to certain cells, especially in the liver and the brain, are permanent.

Late in 1988 a fellow student from a Lethal Force Institute class called to tell me that he had just been diagnosed with acute lead poisoning. His primary symptoms had been extreme, almost uncontrollable irritability, deep fatigue, and memory problems. I am embarrassed to say that I didn't pay much heed to his warning. I did almost all of my instructing on outdoor ranges, and only used the indoor range for practice, usually by myself. So I figured there wouldn't be that much lead in the air. More importantly, I didn't know much about lead poisoning, and I didn't take it seriously. It sounded to me like the kind of made-up malady that it's fashionable to whine about. I was wrong.

Over the next several months, my own level of irritability rose exponentially. This was accompanied by crushing fatigue, constant headaches, intense moodiness, severe sleep problems, and acute memory lapses. The memory problems were the most disturbing, because I had always had a "steel trap" memory. At one point, shortly before I was diagnosed, I spent two days constructing a complex computer data base, and then found a printout in my files of an identical data base, which I had evidently constructed four weeks earlier. I had absolutely no recollection of doing so.

This sort of thing kept happening, and it was frightening. Ironically, because my memory was now impaired, I never remembered my fellow student's warning, or his account of his symptoms. As it happened, I finally found a clue to my malady in a science article about lead poisoning developing in members of a police academy firearms class. I immediately put a temporary hold on my shooting activities, and about two weeks later got into the doctor to have myself tested. The result was a blood lead level of 74 µg/dL - indicative of serious lead poisoning. Over the next 40 days that level dropped to 34 µg/dL, about 1 µg/dL per day, so I assume that it was nearly 90 µg/dL when I stopped my exposure two weeks before testing.

Because my lead level dropped quickly once I curtailed exposure, I chose not to have chelation therapy, which has some risks. As my blood lead level dropped, most of my symptoms vanished. The fatigue endured the longest. I went back to shooting, but I instituted rigorous hygiene and respiration safeguards, and my lead level has stayed down for the last 9 years. I know, both from my experience, and that of others, that the risk of lead poisoning is very real, and the experience of lead poisoning is not a lot of fun.

Anthony M. Gregory, Lt./Rangemaster
Cumberland, Indiana Police Department

4

Refresher on Firearm Handling and Basics

WEAPON EXTRACTION

If facing a lethal threat with your weapon already drawn, the advantage is yours. If, however, your firearm is securely in your holster and you are suddenly attacked by a person with a gun, knife, or even a tire iron, the advantage swings to the perpetrator.

Of course, if your attacker is 25 yards away, there should be plenty of time to draw and, if necessary, fire. Should the attacker have a firearm, regardless of distances, there is no choice in tactics...if the threat is real and your life is in immediate danger.

> Knowing how to shoot is the easy part. Knowing when is the important part.

When called to use a firearm during a close-quarter combat condition, the police officer will, in most cases, have to act in a very short time span. In this tiny window of time, the Law Enforcement Officer (LEO) will have to withdraw the holstered firearm from most any condition (facing the other way, on the ground, in a vehicle, or other contortionist positions) and bring the gun into battery. It stands to reason that the faster the weapon can be brought into battery, the more time the officer has to: (1) seek cover, (2) assess the situation, and (3) get off a lifesaving shot. What the LEO does *not* have time for in such close-quarter life or death conditions is to be looking for a sight picture.

With regard to a fast draw, today's modern weapon retention devices can be mastered with practice by following the holster manufacturer's recommendations. Again, practice is the key to consistent and reliable rendering of your lifesaver. Speed of weapon withdrawal is limited only to the dexterity of the shooter. (Please see Chapter 2 for additional coverage of this subject.)

Sure, we're only talking fractions of a second, but add a few tenths during weapon removal and a few tenths to recognize a sight picture, and soon you'll be wondering why it's you and not your assailant the EMTs are carting off to the emergency room!

All of these procedures are suggested for the off duty/concealed carry mode and are not intended for department uniform holsters that contain security devices. Because of the multitude of different duty holster designs, it is impossible to cover all of the proper weapon withdrawal techniques that these specialized external rigs demand in this text. Those who use scabbards containing snaps or special features to reduce unauthorized weapon removal should follow and practice the training recommendations of their departments and/or holster manufacturers.

In order for the hand to complete its motions and retrieve the weapon in a timely manner with correctly placed fingers, the weapon retention device must always be in the same location. To put it another way, the holster must always be at the same level and in the same location on the belt or shoulder to facilitate consistent draws. Also, the holster must be firmly attached to the belt or harness and must not shift positions.

Your weapon belongs in only one of three places—its containment device, your hand, or the safe place you keep it at home. As you practice the proper withdraw techniques and gain confidence, the pseudo need for premature drawdowns will diminish as will any thoughts of placing your gun in any other location. This lesson was learned the hard way by one large reputable federal law enforcement agency a few years back. During a high-speed chase, two of the plain clothes officers, in separate vehicles, removed their weapons from their holsters and placed their guns on the seat next to them in anticipation of an impending shoot-out. A worst-case scenario developed when their cars were jostled enough during the stop that their firearms were knocked to the floorboard and consequently lost for the duration of the battle. Some of the responding agents lost their lives in the ensuing firefight that has become known as the Miami FBI Shootout (https://www.fbi.gov/news/stories/2011/april/miami_041111/miami_041111).

As with shooting, practice drawing from multiple position and conditions. Master the straight standing position and then as you gain proficiency, from the side step, the turn and fire routine, or other statuses taught at your academy.

All the rules, statutes, restraining orders, 911 calls, hand-to-hand combat techniques, aerosol spray Mace or other pseudo protective measures will never equal the effectiveness of a firearm when faced with an unwarranted and deadly criminal attack.

TRIGGER CONTROL

Trigger control is the science of depressing and releasing the trigger. Please note that releasing the trigger is included in this definition and is of equal importance to the rearward movement of the trigger. Inconsistent release will be most noticeable during rapid fire, as in a life or death gun battle.

The trigger should be operated in both directions uniformly and at the same speed and pressure. The trigger should not stop during its travel other than at the terminal ends. Trigger control is not squeezing! Squeezing is defined as pressure applied to the subject (trigger) by two or more objects (fingers and hand). Only the index finger should move (apply pressure), while the other fingers maintain a constant and uniform tension on the stocks. The classic example used by some instructors is relating the squeezing of a lemon or eyedropper to the squeezing of a trigger. To squeeze by these methods is applying pressure by two or more objects and is not proper trigger control. To correctly depress the trigger, you must move only the index finger and in a nonstop uniform motion.

After the shot is away, the trigger must be returned to its original position. As mentioned earlier, the release of the trigger is also part of the function of the index finger. Do not just take your finger away and thus allow the trigger to snap back because you will then have to reposition your finger for the next shot and your rhythm will be lost. Release the trigger in the same positive manner and at the same speed as you depressed it.

This control technique is very important during rapid fire as well as in *Instinct Combat Shooting*. The use of this depress-release pattern will help keep the firearm pointed at the target during all phases of shooting.

In other words, after the shot is away, control of the trigger release will insure that the firearm is maintained on target and the finger will be no more than a hinge that opens and closes the trigger, making it ready and poised for additional shots.

As with removal of the weapon, constant and consistent motion is required for proficient utilization of a handgun. Mounting, trigger control, and grip tension are of equal importance in the handling of a rifle or shotgun; however, combat handgunning requires the addition of speed. If your life depends on surviving a confrontation with an armed and dangerous assailant, then it is imperative that the aforementioned procedures be practiced until they become rapid and natural. Missed shots and time lost in a gunfight could mean lost life—your own.

PHYSICAL POSITIONS

A substantial part of trigger control is the correct use of the fingers. As mentioned earlier, a comfortable and consistent placement of the hand and fingers is first and foremost. The actual positions and operations of these digits are as follows:

Index Finger

This digit touches and operates the trigger only. It does not touch the stock at any point from its tip where it protrudes through the trigger guard to its third joint at the hand. Stocks that do not allow for a space between the index finger and the gun frame or stock are not properly designed. The pad between the tip and the first joint is the correct point of contact on the trigger. Do not place the trigger in the crevice of the first joint or on the pad between the second and third joints.

Middle and Ring Fingers

These fingers are placed comfortably on the stock to hold the weapon firmly. Pressure and position of these two digits are constant and consistent at all times from draw to fire to trigger release. Memory grooves on the stock will help locate and maintain the correct position.

Small Finger

The baby finger only lightly touches the stocks. This finger has no real value but can cause inconsistent hits if too much tension is applied. Light consistent pressure is the rule with the pinky.

Thumb

This digit, like the ring and middle fingers, holds the gun firmly. The thumb also should always be in the same place, locked low and in a comfortable position. Do not lap it over the middle or ring fingers as this will cause uneven pressure on them.

BODY/STANCE

One of the most beneficial aspects of developing the techniques of *Instinct Combat Shooting* is that there are not rigid requirements for positioning the body, feet, and arms. Some old style defensive shooting procedures required the shooter to assume certain positions with regard to the body or extremities. These set placements worked very well as long as the defending police officer was standing on level ground, facing his attacker squarely and had full control of both hands and arms.

With *Instinct Combat Shooting*, the officer need only learn to coordinate eye contact with barrel position. Other than hand placement, as noted earlier and still a requirement for any form of handgun shooting, there are no additional set mechanical procedures or positions to learn. However, to make effective use of the *Instinct Combat Shooting* method, the trainee should have mastered basic target shooting practices and stances.

Do not learn to rely on certain body or foot positions, as it is more important to be able to shoot accurately from different positions by depending on proper grip and use of the eyes.

Once you have gained proficiency in the methods taught here, you will be comfortable hitting targets from most any body position, including lying flat on your back!

5

Mental Acuity

To recognize what you see;
to see what you recognize.

The mental attitude is one of the most important aspects of *Instinct Combat Shooting*. You must be positive in your approach with the highest level of intent and concentration. You must be convinced in your own mind that the target you are looking at will be hit when and where you want it hit.

The study and practice of defending your life by taking the life of another is a very somber and perilous affair. This is not just an exercise in punching holds in paper targets—this is punching holes that could result in nonliving persons. During the practice sessions, you should prepare yourself mentally, treating your practice as if it were a life or death situation. Unlike bull's eye shooting, you must be "up" and in "Condition Red" as if this practice is a do or die condition.

If you believe that psychological verbiage will enable you to bluff your way out of a dangerous situation, you might be wrong ... dead wrong. Super-predators – losers with nothing to lose – can't be bluffed.

Practice in this hypermental state, assuming you have mastered the afore-mentioned basics, then everything will fall into place should a firefight ever actually occur. Having to consciously think about trigger control or grip will break your concentration and prevent you from keeping your mind and eyes on the target. The scene of an imminent gun battle is not the place to realize that your fundamental shooting skills are lacking.

To be confident of hitting your assailant you must be sure, without checking or even thinking about it, that your hands are locked in proper position from draw to first shot.

Again, this is not a plinking exercise, so key yourself up for the task at hand. Your mind must be focused on survival and not cluttered with thoughts of sight alignment, grip, stance, etc. Also, concentrating fully does not mean being tense. Obvious tension on your part might be transmitted to the perp and thus cause more aggression. As with any police contact, look and act alert and confident in order to help demoralize your opponent.

Be aware of and resist the tendency to "walk" your shots. During practice sessions, the inclination is, if seeing the holes slightly off-center, to move the aiming point to compensate. If the holes are not where you are looking, your grip is not right—fix the problem, not the symptom. The danger in "walking" shots is that in a real firefight, you won't be able to see the "holes" due to the perp's clothing and/or low light. Relying on visual confirmation of scores is a dangerous precedent.

Think positive. Be confident that your training will ensure that your hand will automatically go to the correct position in the same way every time, that you will operate the trigger in the same way every time, and that the shots will all go to the point of concentration.

To keep an advantageous mental attitude, you should run worst-case scenarios through your mind on a daily basis. Alone or with the companionship of a fellow officer or training partner, ask what would you do if you surprised an armed robbery in progress while picking up your lunch at the local pizzeria? Would your gun hand be out of action, because it was holding your wallet, flashlight or ??? Where in the store could you take cover? Did you see an accomplice in the get-a-way car and could he be coming in behind you?

Perhaps the most important aspect of the mental condition of every person who carries a firearm is the ability to justify the taking of another's life. It is assumed that the reader, by studying combat firearms methods, has personally reconciled this power with his or her own mortality and the ramifications of IAD, media, and criminal investigations.

Losing a gun battle is forever; but the aftermath of surviving a firefight, with the possibility of criminal prosecution and civil suit, might be worse.

USE OF DEADLY FORCE

Police officers carry firearms and less-than-lethal tools for two reasons:

1. For purposes of self-protection.
2. To protect society. Ergo, since society allows police to carry these defensive instruments to facilitate the requisites of the job, it goes without saying that officers are expected to place themselves between danger and members of society when so required.

What does all this have to do with instinct shooting? I'm glad you asked that question. Being in a position to use lethal force against another person—intentionally and instinctively—is a measure of the highest level of ethics. Instinctively aspiring to the hero mentality means you trust your instincts—that you are able to recognize what you see, to see what you recognize and act in a legal and ethical manner.

With the best of intentions some police trainers have, in an attempt to save officer's lives, been teaching a mind-set that equates to protect yourself first—don't take chances—suicide is not in your job description.

A MATTER OF SEMANTICS

Perhaps one of the problems is the definitions of words or phrases. Some have interpreted the notion that "LEOs should never act in a cowardly manner" to mean cops must sacrifice their lives for the sake of not being labeled chicken. Nothing could be further from the truth. There is a difference between sacrifice—suicide (purposely giving up one's life to save another) and duty (complying with a moral or legal obligation related to one's occupation or position). An officer's life is of no greater or lesser value than that of any other citizen. However, because of their unique duty they have agreed, by a sworn oath, to place their life—but not to the point of surrender—at risk. In a timely manner and short of sacrifice, a police officer is duty bound to place his or her life in jeopardy to protect members of society.

No one is saying or expecting any LEO to sacrifice his or her life, but each officer has the duty to protect the public. The very nature of the police occupation is centered on dangerous activity. If the work involved only taking reports, directing traffic, and calling in a SWAT team when danger appears, the job could be done by social workers or clerks.

Being afraid is okay. Perhaps the best definition of overcoming fear to perform one's duty is found in the plot and theme song to the early 1950s movie, *High Noon*. On his wedding day, the town marshal (played by Gary Cooper) learns a man he sent to prison is returning on the noon train. The officer is torn between leaving on his honeymoon, as planned, or staying to face the perp. His bride (played by Grace Kelly) begs her groom to give it up. She leaves without him as Tex Ritter wails the theme song—the watchwords of police officers of all time:

> I do not know what fate awaits me, I only know I must be brave,
> For I must face the man who hates me or lie a coward, a craven coward,
> Or lie a coward in my grave.

The bride returns just in time to blow one of the gang members away to save her man, who then out-draws the ex-con. In real life, sometimes the perp wins and sometimes the spouse doesn't come back, but to a sworn police officer, either one of those situations is preferable than being labeled a craven coward.

TYPES OF OFFICERS

When it comes to dealing with dangerous situations, there tend to be three types of police officers: *fools*, *cowards*, and *heroes*. Fortunately, the hero type overwhelmingly represents the American police ranks. In a small, dangerous minority are the others.

1. The *fool* is one who tempts fate by ignoring training procedures and expertise such as not wearing body armor or, for example, not calling for backup when stopping an armed robbery suspect. While apprehension of criminals is an end in and of itself, per se, only

a fool attempts a collar at the expense of officer's safety and when pragmatic options are available. However, that is not to say that anything short of sacrificing one's life in order to protect/save the life of one you are sworn to serve and protect is not part of the job. This is also not to say that bravado is the same as bravery. There is a difference.

2. The *coward* is one who fails to institute a serious attempt to protect society due to fear or a mindset that equates personal safety over the moral and legal obligation to protect others. Any officer failing to place himself in harm's way because of such a mindset is guilty of nonfeasance at best or malfeasance at worst. A coward is also one who flat-out ignores suspicious activity in order to avoid dangerous confrontations. In addition, one of the duties of an FTO is to weed cowards out of the ranks. Of course, if the FTO is a coward....

In response to an article on this subject, one police chief wrote: "Most officers have families, just like everyone else. Their main goal is to get home safely at the end of each shift, and I agree with that philosophy 100 percent." Police officers are not "just like everyone else"; they are the only ones with a sworn duty to protect "everyone else." "[T]o get home safely" might be a great concept for sanitation workers or lawyers, but contrary to what this public official espouses, the "main goal" of a police officer should be to serve and protect the public.

There is no mandate that any officer should be expected to sacrifice his life, but it does mean there are certain inherent risks that come with the badge and take precedent over the desire "to get home safely." U.S. Secret Service agents' main goal, as we have seen in notorious film clips, is to protect the protectee even if it means using their own bodies as a shield. Should they not do so to insure that they can go home at night? Where would we be if, for the same self-serving reasons, American soldiers had forsaken their duty to engage the enemy during past wars? To put it on a more personal level; suppose you're caught in a firefight, what main goal would you expect of your backup?

Any firefighter or police officer who doesn't believe that cowardice is a fate worse than death, is in the wrong business.

The standard that one may use deadly force if one believes he or she is about to be the victim of a lethal force assault is well established in law. This doctrine of self-defense applies to cops as well as civilians. Of course, this belief must be based upon something other than pure fear, such as the perp has a gun or a knife. Even then, being afraid the perp might use the weapon is not sufficient. There must be some overt action or nonaction such as refusing to drop the gun that can only be interpreted as life threatening and immediate. Unleashing a hail of hollow-points without those qualifying conditions is the mark of a coward.

3. The *hero* is one who realizes an officer's primary duty is to protect and serve the public. This American idol firmly believes he or she would rather be a dead hero than a live coward and would shun another officer who acted in a cowardly manner. However, this officer is not the fool inasmuch as this LEO learns and practices safe tactics and procedures. American policing is the standard of the world, the epitome to which all others aspire. We didn't get that way by unilaterally changing the rules of engagement for egocentric rationality.

Except to those who like to make excuses, there is not a fine line between when prudence becomes cowardice or bravado. An officer advised of a man brandishing a gun in a school should request immediate backup and then, without hesitation, proceed into the building. His goal is to find and end the risk.

Anything less is cowardice, nonfeasance, and against all that America stands for. On the other hand, if the officer is advised of a bank robbery in progress, rushing in might be a foolish move. But, not placing oneself in a position to engage the suspects upon their exiting the bank—even before backup arrives—would certainly be deemed cowardice. Likewise, if a crazed gunman opens fire in a shopping mall, public square, school, duty demands drawing fire away from the unarmed civilians.

The prudent-heroic persona should be the ultimate goal for officers. One can teach prudence to the heroic type person, but not the reverse. Heroism, like cowardice, is intrinsic and not readily learned. Self-preservation is inherent in all humans, though, unlike cowardice, it is not over-riding to the heroic type. Teaching self-preservation as a primary function goes against the grain of the heroic type.

THE MAIN ISSUE

Training, be it classroom or on the street, begets predictable behavioral results. All officers must prove to their fellow officers that they are not cowards—that they can be counted on to help a fellow officer under any and all circumstances. Cops must never hesitate to jump into a melee lest they be branded a coward. Civilians, for the most part, are thankful for this machismo as this is what compels LEOs to risk their lives to protect civilians. Besides, if you were a cop, would you want a partner who is afraid to jump into a fisticuff to save your backside?

However, there have been far too many well-documented (some on video tape) Rodney King type beatings. These modern day "blanket parties" are acts of cowardice—actions of police officers who are in reality, cowards, trying to prove their manhood by acting aggressively when there is no chance they will be hurt. Beating the sh-t out of some murderous scumbag might be the only punishment the perp will receive, but it is not, under any standard, an act of bravery. Besides, as justifiable as it might seem, police are only empowered to apprehend criminals—not inflict retribution.

MENTAL BRAVERY

This textbook ethics stuff is all well and good, but what happens in real life when a sworn police officer witnesses a fellow officer violate the law. Does he arrest the offender? Tattle-tale to the supervisor? Adhere to the "code of blue silence?" Used to be the answer was: "It depends on the infraction." If the violation wasn't something major, like a class A felony, and the public hadn't witnessed it, then it was kept quiet or it was left up to a ranking officer. Problem was, just where do you draw the line? What infractions are reportable? Petty theft? Perjury? DUI? Violating a citizen's civil rights because he spit on you? Turning your back, averting your eyes, not volunteering information are all acts of cowardice.

When it comes to police deviance, two factors determine the level of compliance: peer pressure and trust. Peer pressure dates to grade school and is reprehensible when practiced by trained, sworn LEOs who, by their very job description, are individuals. A person who is so mentally weak—cowardly—that he is compelled to go along with the illegal activities of others of his group is not qualified to wear a badge. It's one thing for a bunch of civilians to sneak off the work detail for a beer (or any other reason) and an entirely different matter for professional—armed—officers to do the same.

Trust in the form of reliance is sometimes difficult to differentiate from trust in the sense of confidentiality. Confidentiality belongs to the "you ain't sh_t if you're not a cop," "good ol' boy," "blue code of silence" schools. Not conducive to professional stature, this type of trust falsely conveys a belief that if an officer "covers-up" or keeps quiet about improper activity, he can be trusted as backup when things get really scary. Any professional who stakes his reputation on keeping his mouth shut when he is under a sworn oath not to, is not worthy of the honor of being one of "America's finest." Second, any officer who stakes his back-up support on such a partner who supports the confidentiality mind-set may wind up dead.

Trust in the form of reliance, on the other hand, is of extreme importance to the functioning of any police agency. Cops, being individualists, sometimes need unquestioning reliance from their fellow officers. When an officer's back is exposed during a lethal force or other dangerous situation, this officer needs to know that his partner, his backup, can be counted on to defend him to the death. Being the kind of officer who has mastered the "code of blue silence" is not any indication of how that officer will respond under conditions of extreme stress. The only sure method of determining trust by reliance is the oldest application of trial by fire. On the other hand, an officer who is known for his unquestioning honesty would be the type of officer who couldn't honestly not take risks to cover your backside.

A few years ago when cops were underpaid, undereducated, and selected more for brawn than mental capacity, a certain amount of "discretion" was expected. Not today. Patrol officers routinely earn a decent living wage, and have excellent health care packages and retirement plans that customarily exceed the general population. The substantial amount of ongoing training, education, and certification police officers receive has elevated their status from that of tradesmen to the level of professional. All professionals have a code of ethics. A doctor will not treat the patient of another physician unless referred and an attorney won't have direct contact with clients of other lawyers. The cop's stock-in-trade is honesty and integrity—he must, above all, not compromise these.

An officer who acts as a coward by adhering to the code of blue silence to cover up the illegal, unethical, and/or immoral behavior of a fellow officer must be removed from office.

Police officers are in the business of honesty. This is their stock in trade, forte', signature, persona, identification, and what differentiates them from other professions. When one police officer violates this trust, this code of honesty, all are tarnished. Adherence to or practice of any form of "blue code of silence" is counter to the code of honesty that is part of each officer's sworn duty—his existence for being. The trust each officer has in his fellow officer must be based on the proposition that truth, not cover-up or silence, will save his career. For a police officer or anyone with sworn obligations, justice is more important than friendship.

SUMMARY

The terroristic assaults of 9-11-01 evidenced true acts of heroism. In a feature article in *Smithsonian Magazine* (September 2002): two naval officers, "...turned against the flow of people fleeing to safety and headed toward what appeared to be the point of greatest destruction." At risk to their own personal safety and though severely injured, these officers were responsible for saving lives. This is what America is all about—duty and honor in the face of death.

6

Instinct Combat Shooting

DEFINITIONS

Instinct is defined as a natural aptitude, impulse, or capacity. An instinctive reaction is a natural tendency to act rapidly and with precision without any forethought or conscious planning. Instincts can be inborn reactions, and they can also be trained or learned reactions. We are all born with the instinct to protect ourselves first. Police officers learn to instinctively protect others first even if it means harm to themselves.

Instinct shooting is the action that follows the realization or mental message within the brain that tells you a shot must be fired at a target. The follow-on action depends on your position and that of the weapon to be operated. With a shotgun or rifle you must bring it to a firing position and operate it as many times as is needed *without ever removing your eyes from the target*. This is one of the keys to instinctive shooting. Not only do your eyes have to see the target, but they must focus on the smallest, most centralized part of this target such as the left edge of a clay bird or the chin of an enemy soldier.

> *Instinct Combat Shooting*: The act of operating a *handgun* by focusing on smallest portion of the target and instinctively coordinating the hand and mind to cause the *handgun* to discharge at a time and point that ensures interception of the projectile with the target.

During close-quarter combat, your attention should be—while going to battery—to search your adversary for some small item, such as a shirt button or belt buckle or maybe just the shiny corner of it. This is where your concentration should be and this is where your shots will hit. With your eyes focused at the distance the target is in relation to you, and not on your sights, you will, with your peripheral vision, be able to see any movement that could be dangerous to you. Conversely, if your focus is on the weapon's sights, you will not observe a secondary assailant who might be off to one side—or that your adversary has capitulated.

The coordination of the extremities with the eye/mind affiliation is natural and tasks that require hand movement based on eye/mind information are common to many functions. Throwing a ball is pure instinct. You don't need any sights or other artificial assistance—just look where you want the ball to hit and your eyes transmit the target image to your brain, while the brain computes the trajectory and muscle power needed. Of course, the first time you tried it might have been a little embarrassing, but with practice, it became acceptable. Shooting instinctively is a natural action that also has to be honed and practiced until it becomes expected. Consider the quarterback throwing to a moving target. The speed, trajectory, direction of the receiver, boundary lines, and wind can be mathematically calculated, but he doesn't have the time, thus he instinctively throws the ball with no conscious thought to these myriad elements.

Though the stakes are higher during CQC conditions, the performance is no different than that of athletics where instinctive actions are totally unhindered by conscious thought.

(See color insert.) Incorrect: For close-quarter combat, it is the target that should be in focus—not the gun's sights. Focusing on the sights causes your assailants to be out of focus and thus makes their movement or the presence of a weapon difficult to detect. In real-life situations, you will most likely be looking at the assailants instinctively. However, unless you are conditioned for Instinct Combat Shooting (ICS), time will be lost while you search for a sight picture after determining that a shot is required. Or, if your lack of training results in your barrel axis not being where your eyes are focused, the odds of your shot missing the target will be greater.

(See color insert.)   Correct: With eyes focused on the main threat, there is no need for the ICS trained officer to waste valuable time checking his sights should a shot be required. Notice the sights are out of focus completely, but the assailant's accomplices, though not as clear as the main threat, are still distinguishable. By focusing at the distance of the attacker, the officer can detect other dangers with peripheral vision.

EXAMPLES

Let's take a police confrontation that occurs far too often: You have responded to a domestic complaint/person-injured report. Upon entry into the subject's dimly lit home, you notice the place is in disarray—a female subject is lying in an unnatural position across a chair, apparently unconscious and covered with what appears to be blood. A male subject in a stained, partially opened shirt, is standing in a doorway (normal room dimensions of 10–20 feet), leading to what looks like a bedroom. Loud, distracting noise is heard coming from one of the two doorways that lead from the room you are in. As you blurt out, "What happened here," the male subject reaches behind his back. You respond by yelling, "freeze," while beginning to draw your sidearm in reaction to this overt move that, under the circumstances, could only be interpreted as menacing.

As things unfold, the phenomena known as tachy-interval sets in—a condition that occurs when, under extreme stress, events appear to happen in slow motion. Events, of course, do not slow down, but the mind seems to speed up due to the brain's ability to digest information much faster than the body can act/react. As you draw your handgun, your eyes will be riveted (focused) on the dirtbag as your mind screams, "why is it taking so long to draw my weapon?"

As the perp's gun swings toward you and your firearm comes into battery—the time when hundreds of a second count, do you really want to be looking for a sight picture? Even if you wanted to, your instinct will force you not to take your eyes from this threat. If you are practiced in the method known as *Instinct Combat Shooting*, your chances of surviving this lethal force encounter will be greatly enhanced.

Additionally, looking at your sights under these conditions could be equivalent to signing your own death warrant. If you are focused at arm's length, the appearance of another subject from one of the other rooms could go unnoticed. Your peripheral vision reduced because your focus is set to arm's length precludes the ability to determine if this new subject is a threat, innocent child, or even another police officer.

In the aforementioned scenario, most officers, regardless of their training, would not be searching for a correct sight picture at least up until the time that a shot would be required. At the point of decision, the bull's eye shooter might revert to his training and lose valuable time trying to find a perfect sight picture. Besides, it's just plain common sense not to ever remove your eyes from the danger—a natural instinctive reaction. This book's goal is to hone those natural instinctive actions and couple them with learned and accurate hand manipulation.

Yeah, I know laser sights allow you to look at the perp—please see the "Laser Sights" section in Chapter 8.

VISION

Vision is the reciprocal action between the eyes and the brain. Humans are born with sight, but vision is learned. We are also born with the ability to shoot instinctively, but to be able to *hit* the target, instinctively, under combat conditions is a learned skill. The successful *instinct combat shooter* has learned how to correctly react to the brain's interpretation of what the eyes see. The relationship of the eye to the hand cannot be overemphasized. Therefore, vision and proper hand placement on the stocks, as noted in Chapter 4, are prerequisites to successful instinct shooting. Life and death conditions during a firefight are determined not only by split second action, but by attention spans as well. In other words, if one's attention must be consumed by concentrating on a sight picture, then that time is lost for defensive purposes.

Your eyes, much like a camera lens, have the ability to focus at either close or distant objects. The big difference, and the important one for shooting, is the human eye can focus on larger or smaller objects at the same distance. Whereas, the camera lens cannot distinguish between objects at the same distance; all objects at the same range are equally in focus. The advantage of this selective focus, that humans possess, is that the shooter can focus on the smallest part of the target that he or she can see. The smaller the target you can focus on, the closer to the center of the target your shots will strike.

The disadvantage to being able to differentiate and focus in on one object, among many at the same distance, is becoming a victim of peripheral-optic distortion/dysfunction, commonly called tunnel-vision. This phenomenon occurs when the shooter focuses all of his or her energy of concentration on the target, blocking out of all peripheral happenings. There is a fine line between tunnel-vision and concentrating on the target (more on this later). Of course, if focused at arm's length, the chances of peripheral movement jarring you out of tunnel-vision are significantly less than if focused on the perp across the room. Also, focusing on the target allows you to see, understand, and anticipate his movement.

In the book, *Instinct Putting*, authors Christina, Alpenfels, and Heath put succinctly: "Continuous visual input mediates the interaction of mind and body." In other words, the brain will keep processing information and sending signals to the hand/trigger finger right up to discharge.

PRACTICE

Eye exercises are the best way to keep your sight and keep it sharp. Some basic practices include moving your eyes rather than your head/body when changing the focal point. While driving constantly, move your eyes from road to right mirror, to road, to left mirror, to road, to speedometer, to road to inside mirror, to road.... Don't just "look" at the object—see it—comprehend what you saw. When looking at a mirror, focus on the object and then on the surface of the mirror and back again. Another practice that might be helpful and can be done while watching TV: hold an object in your extended hand and keep shifting your focal point from the TV, to the object, to a near wall to the TV to a far wall.

Tennis players, baseball batters, or other similar sports players all have in common with instinct combat shooters the same goal; this requires the same criteria: they/you must impact a moving object with a moving tool. The tennis player who does not look the ball into the racquet or the racquet is not in the same place in the hand—will miss the shot. Same with the batter and other eye-hand co-ordination games.

Sports play is almost exclusively a learned instinct where the eye/mind/hand/body must work together. One can instinctively throw a baseball, but to place the ball in the strike zone with some regularity, the instincts must be honed (learned) with the established training procedures, knowledge, and practice. Sports such as tennis, basketball, and racquet ball are all one-handed sports inasmuch as they require the independent use of one hand at a time, not unlike handgun shooting. Accomplished players know that to be successful, they must look the ball (eyes on the moving target) into the racquet or glove. No sights are required to pitch a ball, only learned instincts. If the racquet or body movements are manipulated in the same way every time, then the projectile will go to the same target every time. Substitute the word firearm for racquet or body movements and the same principle applies. Once you have learned how to hold the weapon, and where and *how* to look, all of your shots will be on target. But, just like these sports, it is difficult to teach yourself. Expertise in the form of a coach or a book/video/course is required, especially if your life is dependent upon your abilities.

You can get additional practice with an *unloaded* weapon while watching TV. As objects or persons appear on the screen, go through the routine from draw to dry fire, trying to nail the target while at the same time remaining aware of other action in the room or on the screen. Do not strain your eyes or look "hard" at the target. This strain is not normal and will distort your vision and possibly affect your physical condition adversely.

CONDITIONS FOR EFFECTIVE PRACTICE

1. Place tape (preferably of similar color as the firearm) over the sights so as not to be tempted to steal a glance at a sight picture.
2. Be motivated. Don't begin a practice session in a slack or lackadaisical frame of mind.
3. Practice the *right things*. Obviously, repetition of wrong incorrect methods won't be beneficial.
4. Limit your exercises and training sessions to a reasonable time span. Too long creates tensions and lapses of attention spans, which become bad habits.

(See color insert.)   Note: Contrasting tape color was used only for the reason that it will stand out in the gray scale picture.

THE TRUE GRIT—INSTINCT COMBAT SHOOTING

ICS is defined as

> The act of operating a HANDGUN by focusing on smallest portion of the target and instinctively coordinating the hand and mind to cause the HANDGUN to discharge at a time and point that ensures interception of the projectile with the target.
>
> The point at which instinct pulls the trigger is when the firearm reaches battery. The instant the handgun arrives at terminus of extension is when the mind and eyes have determined that a discharged projectile will strike the point of visual concentration.

Training to shoot the ICS method means going from the draw to a one or two handhold and firing at the exact moment the firearm comes into contact with the support hand and these hands reach full extension. From the chest ready position, it is when the arms gain full length. If you train for this pull the trigger at arm's full extension, it will make no difference if the shot requires only one hand or you are in a contorted position such as lying on your back.

The three most important aspects of *Instinct Combat Shooting*:

1. Identify the smallest centralized target.
2. Focus the eyes at the correct distance.
3. Concentrate fully on your target.

If you are a seasoned shooter (have mastered handgun basics and have fitted stocks) and have conditioned yourself to instinctively (that natural impulse) to identify, focus, and concentrate, success will surely follow. Notice there is no mention of using the sights. Handgun sights are for slow fire target work or for distances of over 10 yards. To put it another way

> Target shooting is "thinking about what you are doing." INSTINCT COMBAT SHOOTING is NOT thinking about what you are doing—it is acting and reacting instinctively.

ICS is all eye–hand–mind timing/coordination. ICS is doing what you do naturally when faced with a lethal force threat, looking at, concentrating on, and focusing on where you want the rounds to go.

The difference between being able to place a triple-tap in the same hole by careful sighting, or three shots in a four-inch group, might be your life if the four-inch group was done in half the time as the aimed shot.

> The secret to hitting a moving target is to keep the gun moving and let your instinct tell your trigger-finger when to pull.

Using sighted fire, it is pure luck to impact a moving target with a projectile when you don't know which way the target was going to move next.

Research by Bruce Siddle, in his book *Sharpening the Warrior's Edge*, confirmed the belief that under extreme stress when the heart rate escalates to above 115 beats per minute (bpm), most people lose complex motor skills such as multitasking (i.e., getting into a "stance" [Weaver or other body position] or lining up sights and indexing the trigger). At 175 bpm, it becomes difficult to focus on close objects (sights) and tunnel-vision sets in.

> Single hand, point shooting is the best, most practical means for the military man, policeman or civilian to shoot at close-quarters in actual, not simulated, combat situations.

Col. Rex. Applegate, April 1998, *Notes on Point Shooting*

A handgun that fits is a natural pointer. The reverse is also true: a natural pointer is a handgun that fits the person's hand and persona. If your handgun points naturally, why would you need sights to hit the target your gun is pointing at?

> If one can point a finger, one can point a handgun. and if we can point at something with a handgun, we ought to be able to hit it with a bullet from that handgun. For point shooting to work, the axis of the bore must align as perfectly on the target as the pointed finger.

Dr. James H. McGee, Point Shooting, August 1989,
Petersen's Handguns

The secret to successful *Instinct Combat Shooting* is to let your instinct tell you the moment to pull the trigger. If you wait—even a split second—or shoot too soon—you'll miss. The stimulus is the point where instinct says "now." The only thing on your mind should be that you want to hit the target. Don't think about stance, sights, getting a two-hand hold—nothing except "I want to hit the target I'm looking at—now." If you've practiced trigger control, looking at (seeing) targets, and your grip fits your hand, then your mind will automatically tell the trigger finger when to do it's job regardless of whether you're facing sideways in relation to the target, lying on your back, or any other position.

Movement, especially toward cover, might be the greatest advantage and key to survival in a gunfight. Only the *Instinct Combat Shooting* method allows you to shoot while on the move.

Shooters unable to master *ICS* are usually committing any one or more of these errors:

1. Jerking the trigger.
2. Waiting too long (not letting their instinct tell them when to shoot).
3. Not focusing on the target.
4. The stocks don't fit their hand.

Point shooting is only employed in situations when there is no time to acquire sight alignment and sight picture.

Evan Marshall, May 1998, *American Guardian*

ICS has its attributes and its negatives—just like any other discipline. *On the negative side*

1. It is not of great value at distances beyond 10 yards.
2. It is of little value if the shooter and his firearm are not mated to each other.

On the positive side

1. It is the fastest method for close-quarter combat situations.
2. It is—and this is probably the most significant point—most likely being used by you now. This doesn't mean you are doing it correctly. Of course, if you are already shooting instinctively now, it might be a good idea to understand the principles involved and hone this skill.

ICS is not a panacea—just like the chest-ready position or the isosceles or Weaver is not a covers-all-conditions tactic. The chest-ready position is probably the best of all worlds for most handgun firefight conditions—but not all. There are times when in the real world you might be knocked down and/or not have the use of one hand or arm during a close-quarter combat situation. Also, not only might the perp be moving, you also might be on the move! Hitting a moving target while on the move is the most challenging of all shooting disciplines.

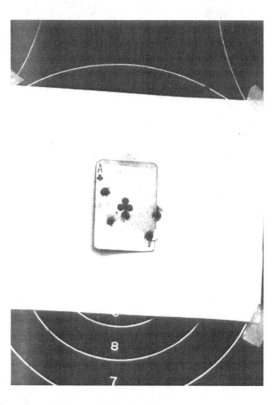

Five rapid fire shots from 15 feet with Taped sights.

(**See color insert.**)   Three shots, three different targets 1.08 seconds **after** hearing the Beep! That's the best I could do, but I've witnessed others under 1 second. Impossible if looking at anything other than the target! Most students at quality training facilities, such as Tactical Defense Institute, are able to get off three-shots in under 2 seconds after training.

7

In Other Words

During lethal force shootouts, law enforcement officers miss their intended target between 70% and 80% of the time (http://concealednation.org/2014/10/fbi-decides-on-9mm-as-their-1-choice-and-have-tons-of-science-behind-their-decision/). This could be the result of spray-and-pray phenomena generated by high-capacity handguns. Officers with 15 round magazines might tend to feel safer firing more shots than their counterparts of yesteryear when 6-shot revolvers were the issue/carry norm. Or it could be due to the look at the front sight training mantra taught in many police academies. Trained to seek a sight picture before pulling the trigger LEOs will do as trained and could, under the extreme stress of a lethal force incident, be so stressed out they pull the trigger as soon as they see the front sight—regardless of where the gun is pointed.

THE TRICKS

Warning: For these "tricks" to be successful, the shooter must be practiced in the subject field.

Causing a bullet to impact the target where you intend is akin to throwing a baseball, dart, bean bag, or other similar eye/hand/mind events. These challenges can be overcome when instinct and practice are combined. The technique, *the trick*, is to not only look at the target but to look at the smallest part of the target while devoting full concentration just before and during release of the shot/throw. This focus on the target is more than a visual knowledge of the target; it is total attention to the target-within-a-target. You don't have to stare at the target, only see it and focus on a small portion of it during the almost immeasurably short time while the body/hand is moving to point of fire—going from the draw or chest-ready position to battery.

Instinct Combat Shooting: The act of operating a *handgun* by focusing on smallest portion of the target and instinctively coordinating the hand and mind to cause the *handgun* to discharge at a time and point that ensures interception of the projectile with the target.

In the stay-alive world, if you see the perp (target) advance toward you with deadly intent, you will most likely be looking at him with your undivided attention. That is not enough. Having decided to engage in a close-quarter firefight, you should—while in the process of going from that point of decision to battery—focus on a small point (button, stain, shirt pattern). This intensity of vision and concentration—at the instant just before firing—will allow your natural mental powers to coordinate the hand and trigger finger to cause the firearm to discharge at the most opportune moment.

All of this needs to happen in a very small time frame, for example, just short of simultaneous.

1. See the target.
2. Decide to shoot.
3. Start the gun moving toward battery (the point where the gun is at its shooting position—usually when the support hand contacts the shooting hand).
4. Focus on a small target-within-the-target.
5. Trust your instincts and pull the trigger at the instant the firearm reaches battery.

Some might call this intense focus tunnel-vision. It is. Though tunnel-vision has been projected as a no-no, it is mandatory during the extremely brief moment when you transition from deciding to shoot to the completion of that shot(s). Of course, you have to be aware of additional threats and the background (innocents), but only before the decision to shoot. Once the time frame of *decide-to-shoot to completion-of-the-shot(s)* has begun, full concentration—oblivious to all else—is required. This time frame during which you are engaged in tunnel-vision is only a matter of milliseconds. Perhaps, world champion racecar driver, Phil Hill, said it best: "True concentration is not aware of itself" (*Car and Driver*, November 1962).

Many articles, columns, and books have espoused the virtues of "watching the front sight" while engaged in combat shooting. If these reports are studied closely, it is evident that the writers are, in almost all cases, relating to shooting contests at inanimate targets. During real life–death scenarios, survivors seldom have the luxury of taking their eyes off the threat to focus (adjust point of aim) on the front sight much less seek a perfect sight picture. The purpose of seeking the front—or any other physical sight—is to adjust the point of aim if so needed. Of course, this takes time, albeit only fractions of a second PER adjustment, but time your adversary has to blow you away.

Shooting for score/time during a close-quarter combat match is a recreation where the danger lies in forming negative survival skills/habits. Shooting to survive should be a self-mandate. Practice what you need to survive and save the fun stuff for your retirement years. It is my suggestion that during close-quarter police style matches the sights be taped (covered) on all competitors handguns. In addition, aerial targets (using paintball, Simunition, or pellet/BB gun) should be included in the contests.

Timing, as they say, is everything. And in instinct shooting, nothing could be more critical. This is the hard part. You can have all the basics down pat, be an expert at mechanical exercises, stare intently at a pinpoint on the target, but ignore the body/mind instinctive reflexes. Having the timing as second-nature will allow hits on non-prearranged targets from non-standard body positions. It's not only about staring at the target or even the target-within-the-target. It's also about timing, for example, a series of motions and actions where the mind's computer—from visual input—instructs the arm and trigger finger when and how to act. The mind computes much faster than the body can react. Thus, it is not necessary to stare or spend more than an instant focusing on the target-within-the-target.

This is especially important if the target is moving. To be successful during a close-quarter firefight, you must be conditioned to instinctively override your preset want to look at the sights.

The human brain has an uncanny ability to adjust trigger pull, arm motion/angle, and other related tactics—all without consciously thinking about it. That's why it is possible to hit a moving target—even with a handgun. As the eyes follow the target, the mind almost instantly computes and directs the course and speed of the firearm as it moves toward battery while giving the trigger finger the command to act at the instant of battery. From another perspective, if the mind is forced (ingrained teaching) to focus and adjust for a sight picture it takes more time and throws the timing off.

Another part of timing is firing the shot at the instant the gun comes to battery. If you've identified the target, decided to fire, focused on a pinpoint, but wait even an instant longer, you will have a greater chance of a miss. This is due to the body's inability to react to the mind's change of plan in a timely manner. If the brain is instinctively conditioned to shoot when the gun reaches battery, but you consciously override this function, you will not be able to readjust to the added conditions. This is because the gun is always moving: Skeet and bird hunters, who shoot instinctively, practice this technique. On the clay bird or hunting field, a shot-gunner shoots the instant his gun contacts his shoulder and cheek—his body moving with the target and eyes having locked on to the bottom edge of the target or head of the bird while the gun comes to battery.

(**See color insert.**)   At battery: Shooting arm fully extended, nonshooting hand wrapped around the shooting hand, both thumbs forward, looking just over the sights at the target.

Flash sight picture, front sight only, indexing, laser sighting, or any form of aimed fire defeats real-time instinct shooting (Chapter 12). Body parts can't react to the mind's ability to make changes at the same speed. Trying to focus on a mechanical sight, look at the target, and then make a decision to adjust or not adjust the alignment takes time. In other words, in that nanosecond where

1. Your eyes have picked the target-within-the-target.
2. Your firearm is moving toward battery.
3. Your mind is coordinating the exact instant to send the message to pull the trigger.

If the eyes send an additional message to realign/confirm the sight picture, the timing will be off and though it might only take a split second to do so, that split second could cause a miss.

Just like making a pitch or basket, shooting-to-survive requires conditioned reflexes that are best accomplished by practice, commitment, and familiarity with the task. However, to successfully and instinctively place strikes/baskets/shots, the player must be conditioned to trust his or her instincts. *Instinct Combat Shooting* is not trick shooting, it's practicing the "tricks."

Instinct Combat Shooting: The act of operating a *handgun* by focusing on smallest portion of the target and instinctively coordinating the hand and mind to cause the *handgun* to discharge at a time and point that ensures interception of the projectile with the target.

In *visual behavior*, the author writes about *doing what we're doing*.

One of the fundamentals of control theory, in fact the most basic concept, is the idea of *feedback*. When information is incorporated into what the system is controlling, then the system can continue to control, self-correct all the way. In order to satisfy a preset goal of a given temperature, the thermostat tells the furnace to turn on when the information 'not warm enough' enters the system and tells the furnace to turn off when 'it's just right'—when the desired temperature has been reached. In voluntary human behavior, *vision provides critical feedback* to all that we do. When that feedback loop is interrupted or only functions feebly, then the phenomenon of 'doing what they're doing' shows up.

Now interject this feedback concept to the milliseconds required from deciding-to-shoot to the firearm-reaching-its-terminal-position and the idea of trying to add feedback into the equation should be clear—it's time consuming—deadly time consuming if you're an LEO facing a lethal force incident. Self-correcting, when faced with a shoot-now situation, is not conducive to survival. If you are trained to interrupt your decision to shoot by relying on visual feedback (sight/slide alignment), then time is lost. Just like the thermostat, if you're conditioned (programmed/trained) to check your sight picture—that's what you will do even if it takes more than a few microseconds.

Target shooting, which most readers of civilian gun magazines train for, allows for attaining proper stance, target knowledge, and other niceties that an LEO does not have when faced with a scenario that might have never been encounter before. During lethal force incidents (LFIs), a law enforcement officer might be required to draw-on-the-drop, shoot from a lying down (as in knocked-down) position or any other imagined or unimagined condition. Shooters, civilian, or LE, do as they are trained to do. If your training is to check the sights or visualize the barrel/slide to the target (indexing) before shooting and you are required to engage a future handcuffee from an unorthodox position or the perp is on the move, that's what you'll do. If, on the other hand, your training is to look where you want your bullet to strike, you will only need to stroke the trigger—as your instinct combat training mandates.

In the stay-alive world, if you see a potential cop-killer advance toward you with deadly intent, you will most likely be looking at him with your undivided attention. That is not enough.

One last look: It's mid-watch, you've responded to an assault call to find a person lying on the ground who appears to be covered in blood. Exiting your shop amid a gaggle of onlookers, you quickly notice a man dressed in black approaching with what could surely be a knife in hand. The flashes of red and blue strobes bounce off the windows of storefronts and parked cars, and there is a lot of movement and noise. You draw your Glock. The distance linking you to this danger suddenly diminishes as the man in black leaps toward you—with what clearly is a knife in the thrust position. Your chances of surviving are significantly reduced if you're training is to adjust the position of the front sight or index a black framed pistol against a black target, at night, with confusing sounds and lighting. At the instant, you decide to remove this lethal threat, you should be looking intently at the center of center mass—or even the human nature response of looking at the knife itself. Oh yeah, and you should be moving. So both of you are moving—are you sure you would want to be seeking a sight picture or looking for a laser dot?

Many police officers and trainers read civilian gun magazines for their excellent coverage of the latest firearms. However, these magazines' training tactics are not police oriented and LEO should keep this in mind when perusing them.

Every day as part of my exercise routine, I practice *Instinct Combat Shooting*, albeit, sans a gun. With my hands at my side, I begin by scanning the room. When I locate a target, I start my simulated draw while focusing on a target-within-the-target and pull-the-trigger as my hands come together at battery.

Instinct Combat Shooting is not for amateurs. It is a concept that requires goals, knowledge, basics of handgunnery, and practice—the right kind of practice. (*Note*: In this treatise, I have referenced the term "microseconds/milliseconds/nanosecond" as interchangeable terms to mean any extremely short span of time. They are best-case conditions. If you are trained to seek a sight picture or index your shot, it will take significantly longer under the real-life stress of a close-quarter-combat (CQC) firefight).

8

Tactical

Because firefights seldom present themselves under "range" conditions, it is necessary to study other criteria. Attacks on police officers under low light, when the attacker is moving and/or using a knife, all push the advantage envelope toward the practitioner of *Instinct Combat Shooting*.

STRATEGIC

Six attributes that apply to tactical firefights.

1. *Time*: The officer trained in instinct shooting who makes the most judicious use of precious time has the greatest chance of surviving a lethal force incident. Searching for a sight picture while under a close-quarters attack is not utilizing time wisely. Well-trained LEOs require 8/10s of a second just to mentally process that lethal force is required. This is a lot of time if your adversary is already shooting or in the process thereof. Add another 3–5/10 of a second for each occasion that the officer checks the sight picture or seeks a laser dot or even tries to find the front sight and the outcome of this deadly encounter is not looking up for the good guy.
2. *Distance*: Putting distance between you and your attacker lessens the chances of him hitting you. That's why it is also important to practice sighted fire at distances beyond 7 yards.
3. *Surprise*: If your attacker does not know your plan of attack and/or that you are armed, you have the upper hand.

4. *Cover*: If time allows, taking cover obviously reduces your attacker's target. Survival chances are enhanced by practicing barricade shooting techniques.

5. *Movement*: A moving target is extremely difficult to hit using a handgun, for you, as well as your attacker. Hitting a moving target while the shooter is also on the move is next to impossible, sans *Instinct Combat Shooting* skills. Please see Chapter 9.

6. *Accuracy*: All advantages of these tactics are lost if you are not practiced in hitting the target under the conditions at hand.

LOW LIGHT

Firefight scenarios under low light conditions are of little difference from full light situations. If you can see your adversary and firepower is required, then follow all the procedures set forth in this book. If, however, your target is not visible, then discharging shots, except under the most dire consequences, is not recommended for obvious reasons. Low light levels render standard handgun sights useless but do not hinder *Instinct Combat Shooting* concepts. Glow-in-the-dark night sights certainly can be of great value at distances greater than the close-quarter combat zone, but trying to line up these luminous lines or dots while your heartbeat escalates and time slips away is not conducive to surviving CQC.

In many darkened situations, you or your handgun might be in possession of a flashlight. Trying to concentrate on where your light beam is pointing or remembering that your light is a bull's eye for your assailant is a burden that is not worth subjecting yourself to. In addition, if your nonshooting hand is holding a flashlight, condition yourself to drop it. Your nonshooting hand might be better used to help secure cover, or at point blank distances, it might be necessary to grab the perp or his weapon if your shots haven't had time to take effect. Freeing your free hand will spread to other situations where dropping anything, ticket book, handcuffs, etc., in your nonshooting hand becomes normal procedure. Causing projectiles to strike your attacker is the only objective in a gun battle; all else is secondary. As former Border Patrolman Bill Jordan succinctly put it: "There are no second place winners."

During low light shooting, the tendency to shoot low is due to the sub-conscious fear of raising the gun too high and thus covering up the target. This, coupled with peripheral vision distortion caused by the low level of illumination, can make scoring hits an unsure event. Other than extreme close shootout distances, it is always best to seek cover or just lay down and pick your opportunities.

EDGED WEAPON ATTACK

Most of the training and scenario examples in this book have to do with firearm armed adversaries. What if the perp is armed with a knife? How much space between you and your assailant is enough? Traditionally, survival combat training is usually conducted at 3 and 7 yards for *Instinct Combat Shooting* and 15 and 25 yards for sighted fire. How far can a man with a knife move before you should draw and fire your weapon?

One significant difference between knife verses gun assault is that in a gun fight, the attacker tends to stay in one location or even move away from the threat. In a knife attack, the assailant must make physical contact with his target and thus moves toward the target. It is this forward move-ment—bent on target contact—that is critical. Other than brain shots, even if your shots prove fatal, the assailant might still have enough for-ward momentum (remember Newton's law of motion) to cause you seri-ous bodily harm.

Tests conducted over a 2-year period (1995–1997) at the George Stone Criminal Justice Training Center in Pensacola, Florida, indicated 21 feet is not enough to survive a knife attack with holstered weapon—unless evasive action is taken. One hundred twenty-eight officers/recruits were subjected to a training scenario knife attack from the 7-yard distance. Of them, only 6% survived. Only these 8 of 128 trained officers were able to draw and fire two shots and still escape the momentum of the attacker. The result of this eye-opening controlled test is that evasive action *before* using lethal force is tantamount to surviving a close-quarters knife attack. In other words, if confronted by a knife wielding assailant, jump, step, spin out of the way while drawing your weapon.

LASER SIGHTS

This once questionable add-on has become a factory option on many handguns and, battery failure notwithstanding, has become as mechanically reliable as the firearm itself. In addition to being very accurate, they create a convincing and intimidating factor. When the situation calls for just pointing a gun at a perp, nothing better will get his attention while making a strong statement of "gotcha." This situation is almost exclusive to LEOs inasmuch as they oft-times must draw and point to make a felony arrest, whereas ordinary citizens, sans the power of arrest, usually have no such reason to point a gun at anyone they don't intend to instantly shoot. Pointing firearms in most jurisdictions is a crime.

However, when the conditions require a very quick—as in your life or his—you don't want to be searching for the tiny colored dot. Of course, if you already have the drop on the perp, you will be looking at the target and not the fixed sights on your gun. Then again, fixating on a pinpoint of light might cause you to fail to notice the perp's hand—or his buddy's—reaching for a firearm.

In order for the laser sights to be effective, you must be at battery and the point of light must be on target—and that's the rub. Whereas with utilizing the *Instinct Combat Shooting* technique, you will be picking your aim point while going from the draw or the point shoulder arms position—you will see the spot you want your bullet to strike before coming to battery, and you will be confident that you know where your firearm is pointed.

If, of course, the distance between you and your threat is outside the close-quarter combat arena, then by all means use what sights are available to you.

Therefore, I don't recommend the use of laser sights for the reason that to become dependent upon them will render the officer at a significant disadvantage when faced with a draw and fire or room-clearing (two-hand hold, firearm down) or from the chest ready position (two-hands, firearm up, and close to chest). During any conditions other than the gun pointed at the perp, it takes time—anywhere from a split second to multiple seconds to locate and react to the location of the colored dot. This time span might seem short and insignificant on the practice range, but if the bad guy is about to blow you away, those milliseconds could mean the difference between life and death—yours.

Laser sights are very good under *certain* conditions. These conditions are moderate distances, low light, and reflective target material. In bright sunshine, they are almost useless. When the target is of a soft, light-absorbing material, such as dark clothing, it doesn't reflect, making it difficult to see. In addition, and even under the best of conditions, it takes time to find the point of light on your target—time that might cost you your life. In other words, if you are practiced in the art of *Instinct Combat Shooting*, laser sights are superfluous and could be a hindrance.

Lethal force encounters aside, laser sights are a great aid to target shooting and practicing, especially for those with failing eyesight. But having to hunt for the little dot—during CQC lethal force incidents—could be lethal for you. On the plus side, probably the greatest advantage of the laser sight, for police officers, is arrests where the arrestee can see the red or green dot on his person. There have been many recorded incidents where the perp immediately curtailed his aggressive behavior upon seeing this dot imprinted on his chest.

It has been proven that people resort to their training—they do what they are trained to do. If they are trained to seek a sight picture before pulling the trigger that is what they will try to do. It's not clear as to what happens when they miss—it could be they are so stressed they subconsciously pull the trigger as soon as they see the front sight—regardless of where the gun is pointed. Most contact distant shoot-or-be-shot situations begin with the LEO seeing a weapon pointed at him/her. Their reaction is to draw and shoot and common sense tells us that keeping your eye on the threat is best. If you're trained to seek the sight picture or even just the front sight, your mind is conflicted and time will be lost as you—at least mentally—focus/refocus from wanting to keep your eye on the threat to seeking a sight picture if that is what you've been trained to do.

9

Moving Targets

This is where *Instinct Combat Shooting* is most effective. Because your attacker just might not stand still and let you line up your sights on him, a little practice in hitting moving targets is in order. Placing shots on an object that is not stationary and whose movement is not predictable is the true advantage of *Instinct Combat Shooting*. Unlike skeet or trap shooting where the flight of the moving target is known and lead and follow-through are the accepted methods of scoring with a shotgun. Hitting a target whose moves are unpredictable—and with a single projectile—is most difficult without utilizing *Instinct Combat Shooting* methods. Trying to secure a proper sight picture by constantly moving your eyes from target to sights and back again while the object changes direction and/or speed is time consuming, dangerous, unproductive, and, for all intents and purposes, impossible.

You should attempt this final stage of *Instinct Combat Shooting* only after you have mastered still target shooting. It is a humbling experience, even for the most experienced shooters. Shown in the photo is a simple device for safely moving targets of various sizes. Clamp or bolt a half-inch electric drill holding a pulley to a post or other suitable fixture. In lieu of a V-belt, use a rope taped together or hollow tubing with connectors to make it endless, and place it around the driver pulley. Extend the "belt" to a second pulley on a shaft, which can be set in the ground. Tape empty gallon sized milk or water jugs to the rope and as the drill pulls the rope and jugs around, they will bounce and dance as they contact the ground, making a most elusive target. Wrap contrasting colored tape around the jugs or stick target "pasters" on the jugs to provide visual focus points. Make certain the ground that you will be shooting into is rock-free and soft enough to eliminate any chance of ricochet, and that all participants wear safety gear and are behind the shooter. When it becomes too easy to hit the jug, try exchanging it for a soda can!

Note the soda can (circled) taped to the rope.

Those practiced in wing and skeet shooting will understand the principles. They have learned to shoot by looking at a small part of the target (who ever heard of rifle sights on a shotgun) and instinctively pulling the trigger as the gun *passes* the target without ever stopping the movement of the gun. That's the secret. Pick your small centralized point of concentration (a piece of the contrasting tape), focus and concentrate while moving the gun past the target. It's all done in one split second movement. Move your hands, arms, and body as one unit. This swing begins with the draw and doesn't stop until after the shot is away. It's all one fluid movement, albeit, sometimes only very slight movement. If the gun stops before the pull of the trigger, the shot is lost. This is one of the first lessons taught to clay and live bird shooters—keep the gun moving by moving the entire body—even if the movement is only inches.

SEQUENCE

1. The shooter is poised at the chest-ready position.
2. The target is released.
3. The eyes pick up the moving target as the body begins to turn toward the point of impact.
4. The arms begin to move at the same time toward battery.
5. The eyes, fully aware of the target, focus intently on a small part of the target (such as the bottom edge or the corner of a piece of tape).
6. The gun reaches battery at the same time as the body faces the target, and the trigger is instinctively pulled.

Do not attempt to look at the fixed sights on your handgun or anything other than the point of aim on the target. There isn't much time as the jug will be bouncing and moving right along, and the point of your concentration will be lost in an instant. But, an instant is all you might have with a man intent on killing you. Pick your point of aim at the last possible moment—as the gun is coming into battery. Don't try to guess where the jug is going to be and hope for a lucky shot and don't try to decide on the aiming point in advance. There is plenty of time; it just takes practice.

AERIAL TARGETS

The next step is shooting aerial targets. If the principles of ICS are observed, it's no more difficult than striking the jug on a rope.

(**See color insert.**) Aerial target shooting is a fun practice—just be sure of your backstop. Here the author is using two clay birds (taped rim to rim) for the explosive effect of being struck by a .45 ACP wadcutter. More economical targets are wood blocks (4 × 4s to start, then 2 × 2s as you get better) and a .22 pistol.

National Football League (NFL) quarterbacks are highly skilled at what they do—throwing a football while on the move to a moving target while taking into consideration many other factors including, but not limited to, defenders, other receivers, defense linemen, wind. Other than the Statute-of-Liberty or hail-Mary plays, they must release the ball when their instinct dictates. Not even a modern computer can digest and compute that much critical criteria in a timely manner, but the human brain can—*provided that the conscious mind doesn't get involved*. Most adults can throw a football, though not often accurately to a moving target, but with instructive practice, a limited success will be gained. You might not ever get to the point of being able to hit an aerial target with a handgun every time (even NFL quarterbacks miss), but with the right instructive practice, you will be successful enough times to be confident it's skill, and not luck.

Aerial targets are as near to tangible lethal combat—him-or-me—conditions as can be simulated. With the target being thrown by your offhand, you have only an instant to see the target after it appears in your peripheral vision and then focus on a speck on the target all the while your entire body is moving in sync with your eyes as the gun comes to battery, and the trigger is stroked. The time span for the brain to acknowledge a sight picture or laser dot and send that message to the hand and trigger finger—while the target is moving—will result in a miss. A miss because the target will have progressed to a different position by the time the bullet arrives at the point the brain told the hand where to go and the trigger finger to pull.

(See color insert.) Note expended shell casing just above the muzzle of the Glock .45 ACP, Model 36 (5.5 gr. Unique behind a 200 gr. SWC lead bullet).

One of the most realistic forms of practice is to stand at one end or the other of the rope/jug rig and as the target bounces toward you, draw and fire while stepping backward. It seems like a lot to do, but under street conditions, this is what you most likely will do when confronted with a deadly frontal assault.

It is during this type of shooting that all problems will come out. If you have not developed good trigger functions and your grip is not consistent, it will be evident by wild and inconsistent shots. Should you regularly miss the target in the same manner, that is, all shots are hitting low, for example, then your grip is not correct. On still targets, it's easy to adjust your point of aim to compensate for such misses; here you will find it impossible. Your gun is not coming to where your hand is pointing. You will have to address this common problem, usually by altering or replacing the handgun stocks and beginning again on still targets. For many people, firearms with factory standard stocks are just "natural pointers." Others require custom fitting or special stocks to ensure that the weapon points to where the shooter is looking.

Hitting moving targets comes down to three elements:

1. Seeing what you are looking at. Your eyes must be focused on the target.
2. The gunstocks must fit the hand and naturally point to where you are looking. The hand must be in the same position on the stocks every time.
3. Whether the target is moving or still, the gun must always be moving. The tactic is to instinctively discharge the shot at the moment

the gun comes into battery (either when the gun hand contacts the support hand or just before the gun reaches its terminus [furthest forward point—just prior to the instant it locks out]). This is not something you have to think about—if you've made up your mind to shoot, the mind will instinctively and automatically cause the trigger finger to function at the most opportune moment.

When shooting instinctively, the signal to the brain has nothing to do with preset body positions. The body, arms, and gun must be fluid and moving. The signal to shoot comes from the brain having received input from the eye and hand position that the gun is in position to fire a projectile that will intercept the target. The brain computes this criterion almost instantaneously and without regard to body position or sight alignment. We've all seen NFL quarterbacks successfully toss the ball while in the grasp of a defender or falling to the ground.

Useful information. But what does this have to do with *Instinct Combat Shooting*? Basics! If you are going to be on the move, it is nearly impossible to use aimed fire. The degree of difficulty is significantly increased when trying to hit a moving target (the man lunging at you) while you are also jumping, stepping, spinning out of the way. Trying to line up sights, or even find the front sight for a "flash sight picture" is not only a time-wasting maneuver, but almost impossible to do when on the move and especially if your target is also moving.

Finally, those practiced in the techniques of ICS will find that under extreme conditions such as the draw-on-the-drop, accurate fire can be realized even before the firearm reaches battery. This is possible because the ICS trained LEO will be focused on his point of impact and commencing fire while the handgun is moving from the holster to battery. The first shot of a triple-tap might not be pinpoint, but nonetheless, your chances of success, a trained in ICS student, will be greatly enhanced.

10

Personal Experience

KA-POW, KA-POW, KA-POW! The sound of the .357 Magnum reverberated off the walls of the family room. I reached for... the remote to terminate the inane slaughter of television violence.

Killing... the room lights brought instant darkness to complement the deafening quiet as I stepped out onto the deck. Now, the only sound to penetrate the solitude of our secluded haven on the shores of Goose Creek Bay was that of a great horned owl and the light rustling of leaves from the wisps of a soft summer breeze.

Complacency and tranquility could only describe my feelings as I followed the planking surrounding our picture-windowed cedar home, nestled among the trees of this 144-acre Hoosier farm. Admiring the view of the Kentucky hills across the Ohio River and its smattering of manmade lights, I walked the length of the deck to our bedroom.

After undressing in preparation to shower, I moved back outside to gather some towels that had been left to dry on the rail earlier in the day. Turning to retrace the two steps to the bedroom's sliding-screen door, I was stunned to see the outline of a man, his feet firmly planted, standing halfway down the deck. A quick glance was all I needed to see that this invader of placidity was about my size, had heavy, dark, bushy hair and... *and* he had something in his hand, *and* that something, was pointing at me!

Having been a police officer and a private investigator, I've been in tight spots before, but standing naked on my own property, this guy really got my attention! With my eyes riveted on the thing leveled at me while struggling to reach the door, I yelled, "who are you... get out of here." He didn't say anything and as best I could see his expressionless blank stare didn't change.

Stumbling, crashing, running into the house, slamming the screen door closed behind me, I saw out of the corner of my eye, that the trespasser was now advancing toward my end of the deck. The thoughts that went through my mind as I raced to the bureau where I kept a gun ran from "Surely it's a friend playing a joke on me and he's going to burst out laughing any second" to "this could only be a sleaze bag from some past arrest or investigation who had sworn to get me."

In what seemed like an inordinate amount of time, I reached the dresser—hang on now—just give me half a second. The muscles in my back tensed in preparation for the bullet that was sure to come as my brain strained to scan all enemies, past and present.

Snatching the pistol from a drawer full of socks, I whirled around, dropped to the floor behind the bed, and came up with the classic two-hand hold directed at the screen door whose frame was now filled by the stranger. The silent stranger with something in his hand.

Again I hollered for the man to leave or tell me what he wanted or who he was—anything. No response. He just stood there in the shadows while the harsh incandescence light from the bathroom spotlighted me. Now I could detect that the ominous object in his hand had something sticking out of it—like a barrel!

I waited, listening, looking for the flash of fire that was certainly only moments away. Maybe the screen will deflect the bullet, maybe he'll miss, maybe.... The years of police indoctrination took hold as I resigned myself to empty my gun into this intruder before I died. I strained to see, almost hoping to discern a flash of fire that would bring this confrontation to a very climatic and final end. My death threat didn't move, didn't make a sound. The screen rippled. It might have been the wind. The hair on the back of my neck stood up.

I had to think, go over my options, form a plan; I couldn't take my eyes off the thing in his hand. Surely this isn't real—too much TV!

I didn't have to shoot unless he shot first or unless I was sure it was a weapon he was holding, and he gave some indication that he was going to use it. Since I was home alone I could even allow him to enter the house, and as long as he didn't try to get too close or actually assault me, I could just play this thing out. I really wanted to know who he was... and, why?

The bed afforded enough cover that I didn't want to risk trying for the phone to call the sheriff or a neighbor—the nearest being over a half mile to the west. Besides the police would be at least 20 minutes away, since there was only one on-duty officer for the entire county. I could make a dash for the hallway where I could hide, but if he shot me as I ran I wouldn't be able to return the favor. Besides he could hide too and wait until I went to bed or my wife and sons came home and then attack.

Half lying, half sitting, still undressed, light shining on me and my legs beginning to cramp, I continued to shout, "Who are you... what do you want... get out of here or I'll blow you away, man!"

My imagination was running wild. Maybe he was just guarding the door so that the real perp could slip in the front and sneak up behind me. I tried to be cognizant of my peripheral vision, lest I take my eyes from what has to be some form of lethal and instant destruction hidden by the screen. I held my breath so not even the sound of my breathing could mask another invader.

Then, still without so much as a word, he turned and started back down the deck. In a flash, I killed the light in the bathroom and pulled on a pair of shorts then ran toward the hall. I don't know why I took the time to put on my briefs, but it made me feel better, less vulnerable.

Reaching the entrance way, I saw through the kitchen window, that he had made the end of the deck. He froze as I covered him with light from the driveway floods while opening the door and again drew-down on him. He was less than 20 feet from me now and I could see what was in his hand. It was a pencil and pad of paper.

He could have been killed. I might have shot him. My head felt hot and at the same time, a chill came over my whole body. I'd had men in front of my gun before, but this was different. I was just doing my job then, this was personal—this was home to my wife and children!

I motioned for him to come over where he displayed a message on the pad reading, "My father says I'm a very special person." The stranger was a mentally handicapped, deaf mute!

Keeping my distance, I put the gun down and took his pad. After writing notes back and forth, he finally told me who he was. He seemed shy, so I invited him in the kitchen for a coke while I telephoned his family who promised to send someone right up. I learned from further note writing that he had often admired our house from the road and just wanted to see it up close. He had driven his car only part way up the quarter mile driveway, with his lights out, and had walked the rest of the way.

End of story? Not quite. The next day I learned that he was a walk-away from a state mental hospital, committed by his family, because he was prone to violence and had attacked people during previous encounters. On this occasion, he had savagely beaten his aged father before stealing the car he used to visit me. His brother told me the family wouldn't have held it against me if I had killed him.

I was relieved that the taking of a human life hadn't been necessary, but I was also comforted that I had subscribed to the old country adage: "The door might not always be locked, but the gun is always loaded." Maybe he had wanted more than just a look, but the gun scared him. What if the gun hadn't been available or what if the kids or my wife had been home and one of them had been the first to encounter him, what if....

Author's note: At no time was I aware of the sights on my handgun and, due to my training—and instinctive need to watch this intruder—I never sought a sight picture.

Incorrect: For close-quarter combat, it is the target that should be in focus—not the gun's sights. Focusing on the sights causes your assailants to be out of focus and thus makes their movement or the presence of a weapon difficult to detect. In real-life situations, you will most likely be looking at the assailants instinctively. However, unless you are conditioned for Instinct Combat Shooting (ICS), time will be lost while you search for a sight picture after determining that a shot is required. Or, if your lack of training results in your barrel axis not being where your eyes are focused, the odds of your shot missing the target will be greater.

Correct: With eyes focused on the main threat, there is no need for the ICS trained officer to waste valuable time checking his sights should a shot be required. Notice the sights are out of focus completely, but the assailant's accomplices, though not as clear as the main threat, are still distinguishable. By focusing at the distance of the attacker, the officer can detect other dangers with peripheral vision.

Note: Contrasting tape color was used only for the reason that it will stand out in the gray scale picture.

Three shots, three different targets 1.08 seconds **after** hearing the Beep! That's the best I could do, but I've witnessed others under 1 second. Impossible if looking at anything other than the target! Most students at quality training facilities, such as Tactical Defense Institute, are able to get off three-shots in under 2 seconds after training.

At battery: Shooting arm fully extended, nonshooting hand wrapped around the shooting hand, both thumbs forward, looking just over the sights at the target.

Aerial target shooting is a fun practice—just be sure of your backstop. Here the author is using two clay birds (taped rim to rim) for the explosive effect of being struck by a .45 ACP wadcutter. More economical targets are wood blocks (4 × 4s to start, then 2 × 2s as you get better) and a .22 pistol.

Note expended shell casing just above the muzzle of the Glock .45 ACP, Model 36 (5.5 gr. Unique behind a 200 gr. SWC lead bullet).

The chest-ready position. Two-hand hold, muzzle up, eyes on target. This is the most advantageous position from which to go to battery.

11

Course of Fire

The following is based on the author's ICS class instruction and course of fire as presented at Tactical Defense Institute (TDI). TDI, located in southeastern Ohio, has been training civilians, law enforcement personnel, military, federal agencies, and corporate security teams in tactical firearms and physical self-defense since 1989. The academy is headed by John Benner, a 30-year veteran police lieutenant and retired Hamilton County [Cincinnati], Ohio Police Association SWAT team commander. John is the coauthor of the nationally used CQPC program and is certified to instruct by the Ohio Peace Officer's Training Council (OPOTA).

The facilities, on 186 acres of rural foothills, include a 400-yard rifle range, three live-fire houses, a covered firing line, and a jungle lane. Contact information is available on-line at their website: www.tdiohio.com or by phone: 937/544-7228.

COURSE OF FIRE

Day 1: Morning

Fit of Grips

To determine handgun grip fit, you will be instructed to pick a target, raise your empty gun to eye level, close *non*-dominate eye, and see if sights line up. Adjustments in hand-to-grip will be made at this time. Before moving to the firing line, the sights will be taped or covered.

The target will consist of nine 1" square feet equally spaced apart on the back (blank) side of a standard silhouette target (see photo).

With a loaded gun, you will focus on one corner of the 1" square and, on command and in strings of one shot at a time, shoot. This exercise is to examine the group. If you are looking at the top left corner (for example) and the shoots are all grouped in the lower right, then it is clear your grip is not allowing the gun to point to where the eyes are looking. If the shots are not grouped, this indicates flinching or changing hand placement between shots. It is important that you not look at or try to shoot the previous bullet hole as is the natural tendency when the shooter is close enough to see these holes. Also, you must not "walk" the shots to the point of focus by compensating in any manner.

Other exercises such as from the draw, at the 7-yard line, double taps, triple taps, shooting at two or three different targets per exercise string, and moving while shooting are outlined in the following text. Of the most challenging is the instructor called shot. Here, you will draw and fire at the corresponding number target called by the instructor such as: "On command, draw and fire a double tap at targets 3, 6, and 1."

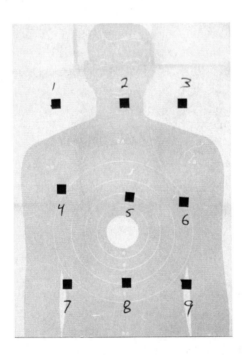

Numbered pieces of tape or target pasters on a blank paper (or back of standard silhouette target as shown) is good practice. When the instructor calls out three numbers, it is quite a challenging exercise, especially from the lying on your back position.

Day 1: Afternoon

All shooting will commence, on command, from the chest-ready position for the first set of exercises.

From the 3-yard line

2-Hands, single shots
2-Hands, double tap, same target

From the 7-yard line

2-Hands, single shots
2-Hands, double tap, same target
2-Hands, 2 single shots, 2 different targets
2-Hands, double tap, same target
2 Hands, double tap, 2 different targets
1-Hand, single shots
1-Hand, double tap, same target
1-Hand, 2 single shots, 2 different targets
1-Hand, double tap, same target
1-Hand, double tap, 2 different targets
2-Hands, 3 shots, backing away; same target
2-Hands, 3 shots, backing away; 3 different targets
2-Hands, instructor called shot; 3 numbered targets
2-Hands, step forward and shoot; triple tap
2-Hands, at a 45° angle to target; triple tap

From the draw at the 7-yard line

2-Hands, from the draw, single shots
2-Hands, from the draw, double tap, 2 different targets

Day 2: Morning, Afternoon, and Night

Moving Incline Target

The target is a 12-inch diameter steel plate attached to and suspended from a pulley riding on a rope. The target, set on an incline, travels (by the force of gravity) down the length of the rope from 7 yards with no more than three shooters on the line at once. The sights must be taped.

Students couldn't see their hits, but even with muffs on, the sound of the "clang" when the plate was struck by a bullet was unmistakable.

1-Hand, single shots
2-Hands, double tap
2-hands, from the draw, 2 single shots
2-Hands, from the draw, 3 single shots, walking with target
2-Hands, from the draw, 3 single shots, walking against target
2-Hands, from the draw, 3 shots, walking away from target
2-Hands, from the draw, 3 shots, walking toward target

Day 3

Moving Ground Target

Shooters take turns, one at a time, on the milk jug moving target as described in Chapter 9. If time permits and you have reached a high level of expertise, the milk jug may be replaced by a quart bottle or even a soft drink can.

1-Hand, single shots
2-Hands, double tap
2-Hands, multiple shots

(See color insert.) The chest-ready position. Two-hand hold, muzzle up, eyes on target. This is the most advantageous position from which to go to battery.

12

Dispelling Myths

Even though focus-on-the-target shooting during close-quarter combat battles has been widely accepted by the police profession, there are still a few castigators. Mostly uneducated and misinformed, they have perpetuated a few myths that need to be addressed.

MYTH #1 FLASH SIGHT PICTURE

This has been espoused by some of the detractors trying to acknowledge the importance of *Instinct Combat Shooting* without actually saying that they now encourage any form of point shooting. Proponents of this ideology suggest that the shooter, as his gun comes up to the shooting position, should somehow establish a sight picture in a flash. In other words, they are saying that all that is required is a quick look at the sights and then bang the gun. Sounds good. Trouble is, what if the sights aren't really in line and the shooter must spend portions of seconds or even whole seconds looking for the correct sight picture? Or it's dark and the sights can't be found at all?

On the other hand, if the sights are in line when the gun comes into battery, why should the shooter need to spend time looking for the sight picture in the first place? Those trained in *Instinct Combat Shooting* will already know that their sight picture is in line when the instant of ignition is required. Furthermore, how would the "flash sight picture" shooter handle a moving target? By lead and follow-through? Come on guys, this isn't Sunday afternoon at the trap and skeet field. Suffice it to say, that at pointblank ranges, *any* amount of time spent looking for sight pictures is time that your assailant can be putting to good use—against you.

MYTH #2 LOOK AT THE FRONT SIGHT ONLY

Yeah sure, like what they've been teaching you all along, the correct sight picture, is one where *both* the front and rear sight are in alignment is all bunk. Make up your minds, fellahs, either the shooter looks at *both* sights or no sights.

First of all, if only the front sight is focused upon without regard to the rear sight, then it should be obvious to even a novice that the course of the shot could be in almost any direction except low. Most assuredly, the shot will be high as the shooter's natural reaction, in his haste to clearly see the blade, will tilt the weapon upward. Once again, time spent looking for your sights will be time that can be used against you, not to mention the fact that under "front sight only" conditions your shot will be wild.

MYTH #3 PROPER SIGHT ALIGNMENT YIELDS GREATER ACCURACY

Okay, you got me there, but only at distances outside the, it's you or me 21-foot combat range. Well, maybe that's a slight exaggeration. Even at 7 yards, most shooters, under match (not combat) conditions, could shoot tighter groups utilizing *both* sights. But we're only talking about a few inches and if you are able to impress a five shot, 4-inch group on the chest of the perp, sans sights, as opposed to a 2-inch sighted group, surely the perp won't know the difference. However, if because you spent even a fraction of a second to line up your sights the perp shot you, then your 2-inch group never got out of the barrel! At closer distances, time becomes even more essential and pin-point accuracy less meaningful.

MYTH #4 INDEXING

The act of bringing into one's realm of shooting the front portion (slide/barrel) of the handgun while in the act of coming into battery. Instinct shooting is not just looking at the target, per se, it is looking at (focusing—intense focusing) on a small portion of the target—such as a button or dirt spot on the target (the edge or center of the "X" of a paper target if practicing on the range). When the handgun comes into battery (out in front and pointed toward the target) is when the mind should have conditioned the trigger finger to pull, pull, pull. Making sure of a sight picture or "indexing" in CQC scenarios is just wasting time—time that might mean the difference between your life or his.

The significant difference between true instinct shooting and "indexing" is the *focus* is on the target—100%. If the shooter is trying to consciously or even subconsciously line up a sight picture or even the barrel/slide of the firearm, then time is being wasted.

As noted previously, during the microshort span of time when a police officer has decided to shoot and is in the actual act of discharging a shot, a LEO's concentration level should be at tunnel-vision level. To put it another way, all of the officer's concentration should be on the intended point-of-impact and *not conscious* of barrel/slide or any other peripheral objects. Taking the time, even if only a split second to "index"—align an object with the target—can mean the difference between life and death. For a civilian target shooter, the difference might only mean a few points of increased score. For a cop, it's his or her life.

Regardless of whether the front sight or front portion of the handgun is in your tunnel of vision, as long as you don't expend any time trying to align these appendages with the target there is no impact. In other words, so what if the shooter can see his hand or anything else in his line of fire as long as he is focused (concentrating) on the intended point of impact. You needn't be aware of anything else, a la Phil Hill's, "True concentration is not aware of itself," observation as noted earlier.

The bottom line is that if you have enough time to find and align your sights, then your attacker might have enough of an interval to get a shot or two off at you. When you have sufficient duration for such niceties as searching for blades and notches, then you have enough time to seek cover. *Instinct Combat Shooting* is for the times when there is no time!

Of course, you have to be aware of additional threats and the background (innocents), but only before the decision to shoot. Once the time frame of *decide-to-shoot* to *completion-of-the-shot(s)* has begun, full concentration—oblivious to all else—is required. This time frame during which you are engaged in tunnel-vision is only a matter of milliseconds.

MYTH #5 FINGER POINTING

Some well-known, but old school, practitioners of combat shooting taught all that was necessary for CQC firefighting was to point your index finger at the target. They usually went on to say practice this method and your handgun will instinctively point to the target. Seeing/visualizing the target was not part of the equation. Worse, under the doctrine of doing what you're trained to do when under extreme stress will produce LEOs pointing their finger at their attacker instead of the index finger on the trigger.

Instinct Combat Shooting is not a one-size-fits-all tactic for all shooting conditions. It is a tool, the best tool, for close encounters of the heart stopping kind, both literally and figuratively. Should you find yourself in a life or death situation where gunplay is imminent and the distances are close, then you should know the techniques that the rest of the good guys have been utilizing all along. Again, this is only for close-in firefights when time is of the essence. For most instances involving greater distances, the old standard of priorities hasn't changed: seek cover first then use your sights.

TROUBLE SHOOTING

If you have difficulties hitting where you look, go back to the basics:

1. Trigger control—not jerking
2. Fit of grips
3. Consistent placement of fingers on stocks
4. Trying to shoot too fast—before coming into battery
5. Shooting too slow—not trusting your instincts
6. Mentally and/or physically tired—give yourself a break

13

Summary

In real life, most shots fired by police at combat distances are, in fact, fired instinctively. Put yourself in the position of just arriving at the scene of an armed robbery. You are instructed to search the area, and during this probe of the probable escape route, you surprise a subject who fits the description of the perpetrator. Your training, coupled with your instincts, tells you to draw your weapon, take a two-hand hold, and point it at the suspect, while issuing a command such as "don't move" or "freeze."

In this situation, which occurs on a regular basis in police agencies worldwide, are you or any other officer out there going to check his sight picture? Hell, no! You're going to be looking at the suspect. In fact, no matter what happens you're not going to take your eyes off a person who may have just committed an armed robbery. Rest assured that if you do have to shoot, you will not check your sights first. You will just fire instinctively, whether you are conditioned to or not. The winners, in these types of battles, will be the ones who have practiced *Instinct Combat Shooting*. Of course, shooting instinctively doesn't mean you will hit the target. If your stocks don't fit or the subject moves and you're not practiced, the chances of missing is greatly increased.

It's safe to say that no matter how much or how little training you've had, at firefight distances, you are going to instinctively shoot instinctively. Therefore, it is strongly recommended that you learn and practice *Instinct Combat Shooting* so that should it ever come down to "him or me," me gets to go home.

Don't expect to become an expert overnight, even if you are a distinguished master at bull's-eye shooting. It takes practice in both dry fire and live ammunition. However, if after a considerable workout, you reach a plateau and feel you should be doing better but don't know why, study this book again.

To score a hit the first time you pull the trigger requires eye/hand coordination taught in this book. To hit the target on subsequent shots only requires adhering to the laws of physics: if all the conditions for the follow-up shot are the same, the bullet will strike in the same place as the preceding shot (cartridge irregularities not withstanding). In other words, if your control of your body and weapon are consistent, then your shots will be consistent.

Use of this method, coupled with a fast draw, is the most effective way of scoring one or more hits on a man-sized target in most any light condition and upon a stationary or moving target. Rapid and accurate shooting was well documented in the excellent treatise, *Fast and Fancy Revolver Shooting* by Ed McGivern. McGivern, at his best, was able to draw and fire a revolver in a quarter of a second. He was also able to group five shots from a revolver tight enough to be covered by a playing card in two-fifths of a second and at a distance of 12 feet. So keep practicing, even though you might never get this good you might become proficient enough to save a life…your own!

Finally, each time you begin a practice session, go over the basic fundamentals of finger placement, your mental condition serious, and, above all, your eyes and concentration on the target.

During my years as a LEO, licensed private investigator, and armed private citizen, I have had to use a firearm on a number of occasions—I have never shot anyone but have drawn and been in the process of coming to battery many times where had the perp not capitulated at that instant a round would have been necessary. In reviewing each of those almost lethal force incidents then and now, I instinctively never took my eyes off my assailant. I can also testify that while holding an armed perpetrator at bay I was able to see, with my peripheral vision, an accomplice and was able to successfully deal with him also. Had I been intent on watching my sight picture, things might not have worked out as well.

The bottom line is your life. If you choose your weapon and ammunition wisely, are able to control your grip and trigger consistently and keep your mind on the subject, be it paper target or threatening assailant, you'll do okay.

The secret to life is the ability to adapt to change.

14

Postscript

Since first refining and developing the concept of *Instinct Combat Shooting* (ICS) and writing about it in a feature article for *Law & Order* magazine in 1971, I have seen it go from question and even ridicule to full acceptance in most police academies.

There has been, and always will be, new and different ideas and products available to those who need a firearm for protection. Some of the innovations such as form-fitted holsters or custom handgun grips have been a boon to police officers.

ICS has gone through a complete cycle. At first, it was touted as the best method of surviving the most common of all firefights—inside the 21 feet battle zone. Next, a few naysayers with their alleged myths about how ICS is not good caused a rethinking of the concept. Now, coming full cycle and with much introspection, the police profession, on the whole, has fully re-embraced the concept of instinct shooting with a handgun.

A few of the recent comments that are indicative of the complete cycle:

I have employees that are very accurate with natural shooting, but very poor with aimed fire due to flinching as soon as they start to look for the sights.

Jerry Usher, *Handguns Magazine*, May 1997

...students were required to fire the standard qualification course twice, first using the "Point Shooting" method and again using "Aimed Fire" technique. Point firing was the clear winner with a class average score of 96.4% as compared to 81.1% when sighted fire was employed.

Steve Barron, Firearms Instructor, Police Science Program at Hocking College as reported in *Law & Order Magazine*, September 1997

...if you can get one fairly well-placed shot into pay dirt, say, three-tenths of a second faster by quick pointing your pistol, that might be the three-tenths of a second that Mr. Badguy would have taken to send a burst of Uzi your way. Instinct shooting may not win the IPSC for you, but it might just save your life.

Jack Galloway, *Handguns for Sport and Defense*, April 1992

Glossary

ACP: Automatic Colt Pistol. The .45 ACP is the caliber designated for the Model 1911 pistol by the U.S. Military for their standard sidearm from early in this century until recently when the 9 mm Beretta was adopted. The Colt .45 (sometimes called .45 Long Colt) is the cartridge for 45 caliber Single Action Army revolver commonly called the Peacemaker.

Action: Movable mechanical parts of a firearm.

Ballistics: Science of the characteristics of projectiles in motion. Interior ballistics cover the time between the start of primer ignition and the bullet's exit from the barrel. Exterior ballistics encompass the bullet's flight from barrel exit to point of impact with a target. Terminal ballistics makes up the study of occurrences after the projectile impacts the target.

Barrel: Part of the firearm through which the discharged bullet passes, moving from breach to muzzle.

Battery: The point at which the firearm is ready to fire.

Bore: The inside of the barrel through which the discharged bullet passes. Size is determined by measuring the distance between the lands—or grooves—of a rifled barrel.

Brass: A generic term to apply to empty (discharged) cartridge cases.

Breech: Rear portion of the barrel, including the chamber.

Brisance: The shattering or crushing effect of an explosive. The more brisant an explosive is the more rapidly it detonates and the greater its relative power.

Bullet: See "Projectile."

Bullet Configurations: HP, Hollow Point; SJHP, Semi-Jacketed Hollow Point; RN, Round Nose; FMJ, Full Metal Jacket; JHP, Jacketed Hollow Point; WC, Wadcutter; SWC, Semi-Wadcutter; FN, Flat Nose; JSP, Jacketed Soft Point; JHC, Jacketed Hollow Cavity.

Bullet Path: The location of the projectile above or below the line-of-sight at a given range. Usually expressed in ±inches.

Caliber: Refers to a weapon's (land or groove) or bullet's diametrical size—usually expressed in thousands of an inch or metric equivalent. Sometimes includes other information to indicated powder charge (e.g., .38-40); or year of adoption (e.g., .30-06) or special designation (e.g., .38 Special).

Cartridge: Cartridge case which contains the primer, propellant, and bullet—a loaded round of ammunition.

Cartridge Case: Metal container into which the primer, propellant, and bullet are inserted.

Centerfire: Cartridge case which contains its primer in the rear center portion. A firearm designed to fire centerfire ammunition.

Chamber: Inside portion of the breech formed to accommodate the cartridge.

Chest Ready Position: Two-hand handgun hold, held close to the chest, body forward, as taught at Tactical Defense Institute.

CLIP: A strip of cartridges used to load a magazine. See "magazine."

Close-Quarter Combat: Lethal force distances of less than 21 feet.

Color Codes:

1. *White* for relaxed state of mind. The condition that most people are in when going about their daily business;
2. Second level, color *yellow*, denotes a higher level of awareness. Anyone who carries a gun should never slip below this level;
3. *Orange*: The prudent person should now be on the lookout for an unspecified, but real danger;
4. Code *red* means a potential deadly assault is forthcoming. You have seen the enemy and he is advancing;
5. Level *black* and you are involved in a lethal encounter.

CQC: Close Quarter Combat.

Crane: Mechanical part of a revolver to which the cylinder is mounted and which permits the cylinder to swing out. Also called a Yoke.

Crimp: The circumferential bending inward of the cartridge case mouth for the purpose of gripping and holding the bullet.

Cylinder: Movable mechanical part of a revolver which houses multiple chambers.

Deadly Force: See "Lethal force."

Double Action (DA): Pistol. Function of trigger pull that requires two actions to discharge a weapon. The first action consists of compressing the hammer/firing pin (main) spring by moving the trigger rearward. The second action is the continued rearward movement of the trigger to the point of causing the release of the hammer/firing pin. Revolver. The first action cocks the hammer and indexes the cylinder while the second action releases the hammer.

Double Tap: Two shots fired in rapid succession.

Dry Fire: To practice shooting with an unloaded firearm.

Elevation: Adjustment to the sights that changes the point of bullet impact on the vertical plane.

Firearm: Any weapon from which a projectile(s) is discharged by means of a rapidly burning or exploding propellant.

Firing Pin: Movable mechanical part of the action or hammer that, when activated, strikes the primer causing discharge of the cartridge.

Flinching: The unintentional moving or "jerking" of a weapon at the time of discharge.

Follower: Movable mechanical part of the magazine that rides over the magazine spring and under the cartridge.

Frame: The non-movable mechanical part of a weapon to which all other parts are attached.

FTO (Field Training Officer): An LEO designated to impart his or her experience on rookie officers.

Great Bodily Harm: (a.k.a. Serious Physical Harm) means *any* of the following:

1. Any mental illness or condition of such gravity as would normally require hospitalization or prolonged psychiatric treatment
2. Any physical harm which carries a substantial risk of death
3. Any physical harm which involves some permanent incapacity, whether partial or total, or which involves some temporary, substantial incapacity
4. Any physical harm which involves some permanent disfigurement, or which involves some temporary serious disfigurement
5. Any physical harm which involves acute pain of such duration as to result in substantial suffering, or which involves any degree of prolonged or intractable pain

Grip: See "Stock."

Grooves: Spiral cuts in the bore that create rifling. Diametrical groove diameter is sometimes used to indicate caliber.

Group: Configuration of shots fired into a target which is used to indicate accuracy of the shooter, weapon, load, or effects of other conditions.

Hammer: Movable mechanical part of the action which, when released, drives the firing pin into the primer.

Handgun: Revolver or Pistol designed to be operated with one hand and without the aid of extraneous support.

Hang-Fire: Defective cartridges that discharge as long as several seconds after the firing pin impacts the primer.

IAD (Internal Affairs Department): A division within a police department that is charged with investigating its own officers when misconduct or criminal behavior is suspected.

Instinct Combat Shooting: The act of operating a *handgun* by focusing on smallest portion of the target and instinctively coordinating the hand and mind to cause the *handgun* to discharge at a time and point that ensures interception of the projectile with the target. Method developed by and term coined by Police Firearms Instructor, Chuck Klein.

Instinct Shooting: (a.k.a. point shooting) Focusing on the target and instinctively shooting any long gun without the aid or use of mechanical sights.

Isosceles Hold: A series of body and extremity positions used to enhance combat shooting with a handgun. Both arms are extended to their extreme length with the support hand firmly securing the gun hand and weapon.

Jacket: Metal cover or skin of a bullet.

Keyhole: Oblong imprint on a target by a bullet indicating projectile instability.

Kick: See "Recoil."

Lands: Portion of the rifled bore remaining after cutting the grooves—i.e., the raised part of the bore.

LEO: Law Enforcement Officer, police officer.

Lethal Force: Any force used for the purpose of causing Great Bodily Harm or death or force which the person knows or reasonably should know will create a strong probability that Great Bodily Harm or death will result.

Load: v. inserting live ammunition into a weapon in preparation for firing. n. a cartridge.

Lock: v. to close the action of a weapon. n. the firing mechanism of a weapon.

Lock Time: Period of time between the release of the sear/hammer and the detonation of the priming mixture.

Magazine: Removable part of a pistol that holds cartridges in such a way as to facilitate chambering them during operation of the weapons.

Magnum: A load or cartridge having greater power. From the Latin term, magna, meaning large or great.

Mushroom: The optimum shape of a bullet after impact with the intended use target.

Muzzle: The end of the barrel from which the discharged projectile exits.

+P: Usually marked on boxes of factory loaded ammo to indicate a high power loading. Cartridges so loaded are not safe in guns not designed to handle these high pressures.

Pistol: (a.k.a. autoloader, auto pistol, semi-auto, automatic). Any handgun that is not a revolver. Usually incorporates the chamber as part of the barrel. Requires manually pulling and releasing the trigger for each shot. After each shot the recoil "automatically" pushes the slide rearward, ejecting the spent cartridge, cocking the hammer/firing pin and stripping a fresh cartridge from the magazine for insertion into the chamber. This action/reaction does not disengage the sear which can only be done by releasing the trigger. Fully automatic weapons such as machine guns or submachine guns will continue to fire as long as the trigger is depressed or until either the trigger is released or the magazine is emptied.

Point Blank Range: Distance so close that appreciable deviation of line of flight is negligible.

Point Shooting: See "Instinct shooting."

Point Shoulder Arms: When the firearm is extended to shoulder level and in battery.

Primer: Detonating mixture structured to ignite propellant when struck a sharp blow as from a firing pin.

Projectile: The missile only. The part of the cartridge that separates, exits from the muzzle and impacts on the target.

Recoil: The kinetic energy reaction of the expanding, burning propellant as it pushes the projectile through the bore. This is evidenced by the rearward thrust of the weapon against the shooter's hand/body.

Revolver: A multi-shot handgun, utilizing a revolving cylinder as a cartridge receptacle.

Rifling: Parallel spiral groves cut into the bore to impart spin on the projectile. This spin aids in stabilizing the bullet in flight which greatly improves accuracy. This rifling also marks the bullet as it passes through the bore. These engravings (fingerprints) are unique to that particular bore and bullet.

Rimfire: Cartridge case which contains its primer in the rear rim portion. A firearm designed to fire rimfire ammunition.

Safety: Any device or mechanism which locks or blocks the trigger, hammer and/or sear to prevent unintentional discharge.

Sear: Mechanical part of the action of a firearm which functions between the trigger and the hammer; acts as a release when the trigger is fully depressed.

Semi-Automatic: See "Pistol."

Silencer: See "Sound suppressor."

Single Action: Only one action is required to fire the weapon such as moving the trigger rearward to release the hammer/firing pin.

Slide: On semi-automatic weapons, the movable mechanical device that functions to extract spent cases and insert loaded cartridges.

Snub-Nose: Slang term which usually refers to any short barreled revolver.

Sound Suppressor: Device which, when fitted to the muzzle end of a weapon, absorbs sound. Sound of the discharge is suppressed, not silenced. Usually installed on pistols because revolvers will "leak" sound at the barrel/cylinder gap thus defeating the purpose of the suppressor. Bullets which exceed the speed of sound can produce in-flight sonic booms that also defeat the purpose of a suppressor.

Speed-Loader: Mechanical device that facilitates the loading of a magazine or cylinder.

Stock: Portion of the weapon which is held in the hand.

Tachy-Interval: A time-deception phenomena. A condition that occurs when, under extreme stress, events appear to happen in slow motion. Events, of course, do not slow down, but the mind seems to speed up due to the brain's ability to digest information much faster than the body can act/react. Many people who have been in serious auto accidents or gun fights have experienced this condition.

Tinnitus: Noise induced hearing loss, often accompanied by a ringing sound in the ears. Common problem encountered by shooters who fail to wear hearing protection.

Trajectory: The parabolic path of a projectile in flight from muzzle to impact.

Trigger: Movable mechanical device designed to be operated by the index finger for double action or single action mode depending on type of firearm.

Tunnel-Vision: Peripheral-optic distortion/dysfunction. A phenomenon that can occur during high concentration where one sees (is aware of) only the center of his or her attention. This temporary occurrence renders the victim oblivious to surrounding events.

Velocity: Speed of a projectile. Usually measured in feet per second.

Wadcutter: Flat-topped and sharp shouldered bullet designed to punch clean round holes in paper targets to facilitate scoring.

Windage: Adjustment to the sights of a weapon to change point of bullet impact on the horizontal plane.

Yoke: See "Crane."

Zero: Term meaning the combination of sight adjustment and cartridge selection that yields a satisfactory group at a desired distance.

EPILOGUE

Our last line of defense: The American Police Officer

Abraham Lincoln was the first to honor *The Brave Men* [and women], *Living and Dead, who Struggled Here*, and in the Caribbean, Korea, Vietnam, The Gulf and *Over There* twice. Now we can add to that the everyday police officers, killed in the line of duty—may they not have died in vain.

Today, on every level we find obese and incestuous government so entrenched that its elected and bureaucratic officials, twist, spin, violate, and ignore, with impunity, the mandate: *Shall be Bound by Oath or Affirmation, to Support this Constitution.*

In the 200-plus years that we've been a republic, tyrannical provisions, never intended by those who wrote about *Unalienable Rights*, have become commonplace. Self-reliance threatens to evolve into protect-us-from-ourselves laws and political correctness is expunging constitutional correctness offending all who have ever pledged, *...One Nation...with Liberty and Justice for All.*

The ideal, the backbone of our very existence, to *Form a More Perfect Union, Establish Justice...and Secure the Blessings of Liberty,* may be failing.

If we are witnessing the dawn of the fall of the American empire because those who are enjoying *life* and pursuing *happiness* at the expense of *liberty*, we will be forced to fall back upon our last line of defense and they will not fail us... and, *this Nation, Shall* not *Perish from the Earth.*

Material Safety Data Sheet
Remington Arms
POB 700
870 Remington Road
Madison, NC 27025-0700
1-800/243-9700

Bibliography

Applegate, R., *Kill or Get Killed*, Paladin Press, Inc., Boulder, CO, 1976.

Askins, C., Jr., *The Art of Handgun Shooting*, A.S. Barnes, New York, 1941.

Barsan, M. and A. Miller, NOISCH Health Hazard Evaluation report, U.S. Department of Health & Human Services, FBI Academy, HETA 91-0346-2572, April 1996.

Cassidy, W.L., *Quick or Dead*, Paladin Press, Inc., Boulder, CO, 1993.

Fairbairn, W.E. and E.A. Sykes, *Shooting to Live*, Paladin Press, Inc., Boulder, CO, 1987.

Fawcett, B., *Instinctive Shooting*, Skyhorse Publishing, New York, 2013.

Goldberg, R.L. et al., Lead exposure at uncovered outdoor firing ranges, *Journal of Occupational Medicine*, 33(6), June 1991, 718–719.

Heath, C., B. Christina, and E. Alpenfels, *Instinct Putting*, Gotham Books, New York, 2008.

Jennings, M., *Instinct Shooting*, Dodd, Mead & Company, New York, 1965.

Jones, B., *Visual Behavior*, Lockwood Press, Cincinnati, OH, 1995.

Jordan, B., *No Second Place Winner*, ASIN: B000V0Y9WY.

Lanphear, B.P., C. Howard, S. Eberly, P. Auinger, J. Kolassa, M. Weitzman, S.J. Schaffer, and K. Alexander, Primary prevention of childhood lead exposure: A randomized trial of dust control, *Pediatrics*, 103(4), April 1999, 772–777.

McGivern, Ed., *Fast and Fancy Revolver Shooting*, Follett Publishing Company, Chicago, IL, 1938.

Seiderman, A.S. and S.E. Marcus, *20/20 is Not Enough*, Alfred A. Knopf, New York, 1989.

Siddle, B., *Sharpening the Warrior's Edge: The Psychology and Science of Training*, PPCT Research Publications, Belleville, IL, 1995.

Smith & Wesson, https://www.smith-wesson.com.

Spaulding, D., *Handgun Combatives*, Looseleaf Law Publications, Inc., Flushing, NY, 2002.

Tactical Defense Institute, West Union, OH.

Weston, P.B., *Combat Shooting for Police*, Library of Congress Catalog Card Number: 60-12679, Charles C Thomas, Publisher, Springfield, IL, 1970.

Index